MA-KA-TAI-ME-SHE-KIA-KIAK.
BLACK HAWK.

ANTOINE LeCLAIRE.

BLACK HAWK'S AUTOBIOGRAPHY

THROUGH THE INTERPRETATION OF
ANTOINE LECLAIRE

J. B. Patterson
Amanuensis and Editor of the First Edition

AN INTRODUCTION AND NOTES,
CRITICAL AND HISTORICAL
BY
James D. Rishell

HERITAGE BOOKS
2024

HERITAGE BOOKS
AN IMPRINT OF HERITAGE BOOKS, INC.

Books, CDs, and more—Worldwide

For our listing of thousands of titles see our website
at
www.HeritageBooks.com

A Facsimile Reprint
Published 2024 by
HERITAGE BOOKS, INC.
Publishing Division
5810 Ruatan Street
Berwyn Heights, MD 20740

Copyright © 1912 J. G. Huntoon

Originally published:
Rock Island, Illinois
American Publishing Company
1912

— Publisher's Notice —
In reprints such as this, it is often not possible to remove blemishes from the original. We feel the contents of this book warrant its reissue despite these blemishes and hope you will agree and read it with pleasure.

International Standard Book Number
Paperbound: 978-0-7884-5124-9

CONTENTS

CHAPTER I.
PAGE

Birth of Black Hawk—Nanamakee Dreams—Champlain—The White Man Arrives—Traditions of the Sacs—The Alliance with the Foxes—The Founding of Saukenauk—Many Adventures.................................13-17

CHAPTER II.

The Louisiana Purchase—How the Indians Liked It—Pike's Visit—The Cession of 1804—"The Beginning of All Our Serious Troubles"—Covering the Blood—A Dreadful Ball Game...18-23

CHAPTER III.

War of 1812—Madison Urges Indian Neutrality—Why the Sacs Joined the British—Forts Meigs and Stephenson—Black Hawk Leaves the British Army...............24-31

CHAPTER IV.

Black Hawk Disapproves American and British Warfare—How Keokuk Became Chief—Battle of the Sink-hole—Adventures..32-42

CHAPTER V.

British Strategy—Battle at Campbell's Island—Defeat of General Taylor at the Mouth of Rock River—A Temperance Indian's Dream of Snakes...................43-49

CHAPTER VI.

Black Hawk Touches the Goose Quill—Indian Ideas of Ethics—Fort Armstrong Built on Rock Island—The Good Spirit That Lived in a Cave....................50-55

CHAPTER VII.

The Watch Tower—The Beauty of the Country—Why the Indians Loved It—Bitter Reflections—Indian Customs—Courtship and Marriage Customs Among the Sacs—Indian Games and Dances—How the Corn Came—An Indian Love Tragedy—Death of Black Hawk's Children—Rendition of an Indian Murderer—Depredations of the Whites...............................56-61

iv   CONTENTS

CHAPTER VIII.

The Sauks Notified to Leave Saukenauk—A Divided People—Judge Pence Takes Possession of Black Hawk's Wigwam—Indian Ideas of Land Titles—More White Depredations—Colonel Davenport Buys the Watch Tower—Black Hawk's Opinion of American Justice..........62-74

CHAPTER IX.

A Gloomy Winter—Black Hawk Interviews General Gaines—The Destruction of Saukenauk—Black Hawk Again Touches the Goose Quill............................75-82

CHAPTER X.

Neapope (Nawpope) Goes on a Mission to Malden—Returns Badly Advised—Pow-e-Sheek, the Prophet of the Winnebagoes, Gives Bad Advice—General Jackson Refuses Compromise—Black Hawk Begins War—Coldly Received by the Winnebagoes and Pottawattomies—Disillusioned, He Decides to Surrender—His Flag Bearers Murdered—Stillman's Defeat................83-93

CHAPTER XI.

The Indians Flee Toward the Four Lakes—Various Battles—Massacre of the Hall and Davis Families—Battle at Wisconsin Heights—The Massacre of the Indians at the Mouth of the Bad Axe........................94-106

CHAPTER XII.

Black Hawk Surrenders—Goes to Jefferson Barracks in Charge of Jefferson Davis—Black Hawk and His Party Ordered to Go to Washington.....................107-116

CHAPTER XIII.

Starts on His Famous Tour—Visits the Great Villages of the East—His Enthusiastic Reception—Sees the Railroads—Amazed at a Balloon Ascension—Recuperates at Fortress Monroe—Surprised to Find so Many Villages and People... 117-127

CHAPTER XIV.

Starts for His Own Country with Major Garland—Meets Keokuk at Fort Armstrong—Offended by Major Garland—His Solution of the Slavery Question—His Views on Various Matters—His Farewell Message to the American People................................... 128-133

LIST OF ILLUSTRATIONS

	PAGE
Black Hawk and Antoine LeClaire	Frontispiece
"A Favorable Report of the Country"—Looking South from the Watch Tower	18
"One Boat Went Ashore"—Battleground at Campbell's Island	49
"On Its Highest Point Was Our Watch Tower"—Watch Tower	70
"At the Foot of the Rapids on Rock River"	62
Bird's-Eye View of Rock Island Arsenal	128
At Nam-e-qua Creek	82
Bathing Beach at Campbell's Island—West End of Battleground	151
General Map of Black Hawk's Exploits, Showing also Enclosed in Heavy Lines the Cession of 1804	12
Map of the Watch Tower Grounds	68
Map of Black Hawk's Home Land, Showing Relative Locations of Davenport, Rock Island, the Watch Tower, Campbell's Island, etc.	53

NE-KA-NA-WEN

MA-NE-SE-NO OKE-MAUT WAP-PI MA-QUAI.

WA-TA-SAI WE-YEU,

Ai nan-ni ta co-si-ya-quai, na-katch ai she-ke she-he-nack, hai-me-ka-ti ya-quai ke-she-he-nack, ken-e-chawe-he-ke kai-pec-kien a-cob, ai-we-ne-she we-he-yen; ne-wai-ta-sa-mak ke-kosh-pe kai-a-poi qui-wat. No-ta-wach-pai pai-ke se-na-mon nan-ni-yoo, ai-ke-kai na-o-pen. Ni-me-to sai-ne-ni-wen, ne-ta-to-ta ken ai mo-he-man ta-ta-que, ne-me-to-sai-ne-ne-wen.
Nin-a-kai-ka poi-pon-ni chi-cha-yen, kai-ka-ya ha-ma-we pa-she-to-he-yen. Kai-na-ya kai-nen-ne-naip, he-nok ki-nok ke-cha-kai-ya, pai-no-yen ne-ket-te-sim-mak o-ke-te-wak ke-o-che, me-ka ti-ya-quois na-kach mai-quoi, a-que-qui pa-che-qui ke-kan-ni ta-men-nin. Ke-to-ta we-yen, a-que-ka-ni-co-te she-tai-hai yen, nen, chai-cha-me-co kai-ke-me-se ai we-ke ken-ne-ta-mo-wat ken-na-wa-ha-o ma-co-qua-yeai-quoi. Ken-wen-na ak-che-man wen-ni-ta-hai ke-men-ne to-ta-we-yeu, ke-kog-hai ke-ta-shi ke-kai na-we-yen, he-na-cha wai-che-we to-mo-nan, ai pe-che-qua-chi mo-pen ma-me-co, mai-che-we-ta na-mo-nan, ne-ya-we-nan qui-a-ha-wa pe-ta-kek, a que-year tak-pa-she-qui a-to-ta-mo-wat, chi-ye-tuk he-ne cha-wai-chi he-ni-nan ke-o-chi-ta mow-ta-swee-pai che-qua-que.
He-ni-cha-hai poi-kai-nen na-na-so-si-yen, ai o-sa-ke-we-yen, ke-pe-me-kai-mi-kat hai-nen hac-yai na-na-co-si-peu, nen-a-akai-ne co-ten ne-co-ten ne-ka chi-a-quoi ne-me-cok me-to-sai ne-ne wak-kai ne-we-yen-nen, kai-shai ma-ni-to-ke ka-to-me-nak ke-wa-sai- he-co-wai mi-a-me ka-chi pai-ko-tai-hear-pe kai-cee wa-wa kia he-pe ha-pe-nach-he-cha, na-na-ke-na-way ni-taain ai we-pa-he-wea to-to-na ca, ke-to-ta-we-yeak, he-nok, mia-ni ai she-ke-ta ma-ke-si-yen, nen-a-kai na-co-ten ne-ka-he-nen e-ta-quois, wa-toi-na-ka che-ma-ke-keu na-ta-che tai-hai-ken ai mo-co-man ye-we-keu ke-to-towe. E-nok ma-ni-hai she-ka-ta- ma ka-si-yen, wen-e-cha-hai nai-ne-mak, mai-ko-ten ke ka-cha ma-men-na-tuk we-yowe, keu-ke-nok ai she-me ma-na-ni ta-men-ke-yowe.

MA-KA-TAI-ME-SHE-KIA-KIAK

Ma-taus-we Ki-sis, 1833.

DEDICATION

(Translation.)

To Brigadier General H. Atkinson:

SIR:—The changes of fortune and vicissitudes of war made you my conqueror. When my last resources were exhausted, my warriors worn down with long and toilsome marches, we yielded, and I became your prisoner.

The story of my life is told in the following pages; it is intimately connected and in some measure identified with a part of the history of your own; I have, therefore, dedicated it to you.

The changes of many summers have brought old age upon me, and I cannot expect to survive many moons. Before I set out on my journey to the land of my fathers, I have determined to give my motives and reasons for my former hostility to the whites, and to vindicate my character from misrepresentation. The kindness I received from you whilst a prisoner of war, assures me that you will vouch for the facts contained in my narrative, so far as they came under your observation.

I am now an obscure member of a nation that formerly honored and respected my opinions. The pathway to glory is rough, and many gloomy hours obscure it. May the Great Spirit shed light on yours; and that you may never experience the humility that the power of the American government has reduced me to, is the wish of him who, in his native forests, was once as proud and bold as yourself.

BLACK HAWK.

10th moon, 1833.

INTRODUCTION

In August, 1833, after Black Hawk's return to the Mississippi from his compulsory, but, as the event proved most gratifying tour of the Eastern States, he called upon Mr. Antoine LeClaire, the official interpreter for the Sac and Fox agency at Rock Island, and expressed a desire to have the history of his life written and published. With this request Mr. LeClaire willingly complied, and selected Mr. J. B. Patterson as his amanuensis. Both men were well prepared for the work they had so generously undertaken.

The father of Mr. LeClaire was a French Canadian trader; his mother, the daughter of a Pottawattomie chief; the twain having been in their youth married under the rites of the Catholic Church, to which both belonged. In 1808, the elder LeClaire established a trading-post on the site of Milwaukee, and shortly afterwards was associated with John H. Kinzie in the post at Chicago. About 1813 Antoine was sent to school at St. Louis, and five years later received the appointment of United States Interpreter for the Sac and Fox agency at Rock Island, under Colonel George Davenport. At the time this book was written Mr. LeClaire was about 36 years old. In all the negotiations and controversies between the white settlers and the Sac and Fox Indians, he had been for more than fifteen years the trusted medium of communication. His portrait, published as a frontispiece, is from the oil-painting in the court house at Davenport, Iowa.

Mr. Patterson was a newspaper man of considerable experience and high personal character on what was then the frontier, and had served as a private in the Black

INTRODUCTION ix

Hawk war. The style of the autobiography is, in the main, simple and unaffected, admirably adapted to the story he was called upon to transcribe. The present editor has taken no liberties with the original text other than to break it up into convenient chapters, and to correct a few obvious defects in the English. The first edition was published in 1834, with Mr. Patterson as editor.

It would be difficult to characterize Black Hawk; nor is the historian called upon to attempt it. He here tells his own story, and by it he must be known. It is sufficient to say that he was a true type of the American Indian; always foremost on the warpath and the chase; learned in every trick of ambush and attack, terribly deft with the bow and arrow, the rifle, the spear, and the tomahawk. His faults and his virtues were those of his race strongly emphasized in him. As a warrior and leader of his men in actual combat, he probably had no superior among the red men; as a statesman and organizer, he ranks below Tecumseh and Pontiac. As an orator and politician, he was surpassed by Keokuk.

Yet two facts stand sharply outlined which must preserve his name through the whole course of American history:

Besides the engaging stories of Indian life and adventure here related, he has given us in his autobiography the closest and most intimate view ever had of the Indian mind. Those wild, mysterious people, lurking in the forest or below the horizon, have made themselves known to civilized man chiefly by the sharp inscription of the scalping knife. Catlin, Schoolcraft, Atwater, and other intelligent and truthful writers in plenty, have sat down in their wigwams and council lodges and, bewildered strangers among these uncommunicative people, have gone home to tell what they saw and to record the conclusions of their own minds. Yet, because they were of a widely divergent race, heirs of entirely different customs and habits of thought, the incomprehensible Indian remained only a little less mysterious than before. On every page, Black Hawk, quite unconscious of the gift rendered, reveals the highly individuated Indian race.

It is to be regretted that there is no other book in existence with this peculiar ethnic quality, nor can there be another. It would be most entertaining and instructive to study this subject from other viewpoints of Indian experience and temperament; but the last Indian unmodified by the white man's schools, permanent and convenient markets, close contact, and other strong influences of civilization, has passed away. The unique character of Black Hawk's autobiography, therefore, assures him an enduring place in our annals and gratitude.

The other distinctive claim which Black Hawk makes upon posterity is the war which bears his name. Now, that war is of little military significance. It called into the field a remarkable number of men destined in later years to impress themselves indelibly upon our history; for example, Gen. Edmund P. Gaines, Gen. Henry Atkinson, Major Robert Anderson, Abraham Lincoln, Jefferson Davis, Gen. Zachary Taylor, and others only less renowned; but not one battle added luster to American arms. There were many examples of splendid courage and manly steadfastness; but the affair as a whole was marked by mismanagement, insubordination, and panic; and this is equally true of the Indians and the Americans. The one strictly military feat of a notable character was that at Wisconsin Heights, where Black Hawk, with admirable generalship, held back the troops under Generals Henry and Dodge, until the women and children of his tribe could escape across the Wisconsin River. They escaped only, however, to be met at the mouth of the Bad Axe and relentlessly massacred.

INTRODUCTION

But the Black Hawk war will be forever memorable as marking the end of an epoch. It was the last stand of the Indian tribes in the old Northwest. The thrilling story of that vast and wonderful land, for whose possession the French, the English, the Indians, and the Americans, had waged a New World Hundred Years' War, had its culmination at the Bad Axe. Here the fierce wrath of the American troops, reflecting the exhausted patience of the pioneers, went far towards squaring the long and bloody account between the white man and his red brother.

JAMES D. RISHELL.

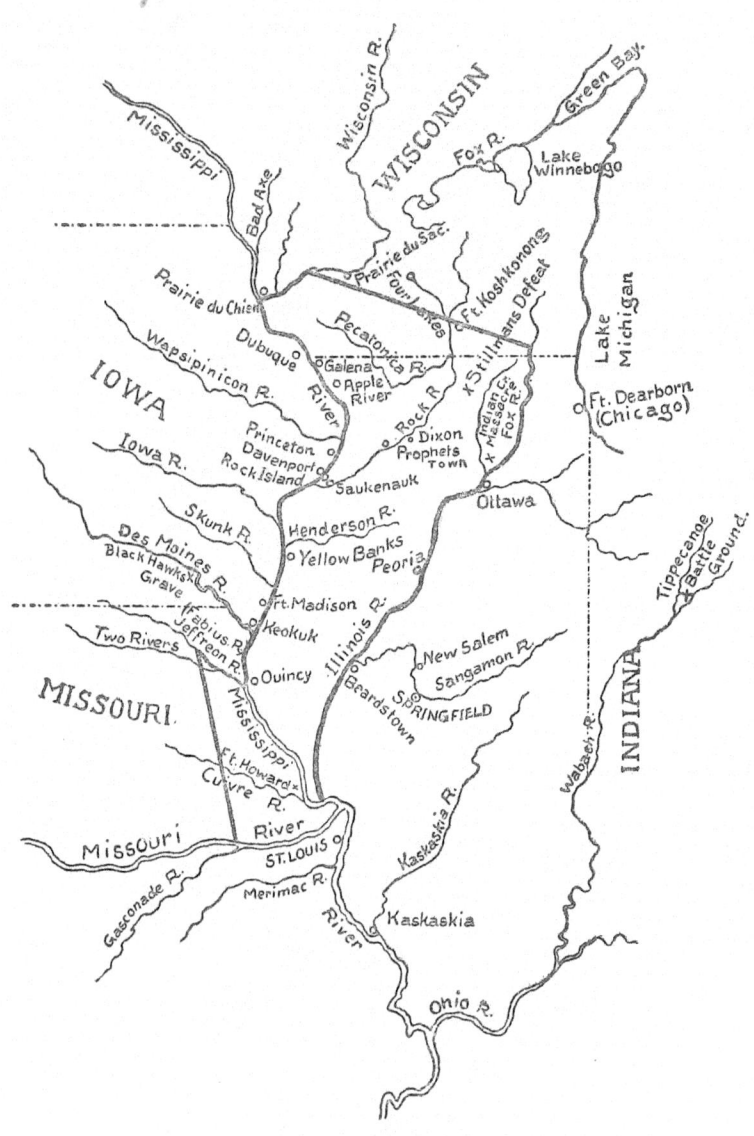

AUTOBIOGRAPHY OF BLACK HAWK

CHAPTER I.

BIRTH—TRADITIONS OF THE SACS—CHAMPLAIN—THE GREAT SPIRIT INSTRUCTS THE SACS.

I was born at the Sac village on Rock River (1) in the year 1767, and am now in my 67th year. My great-grandfather, Nanamakee, or Thunder, according to the tradition given me by my father, Py-e-sa, was born in the vicinity of Montreal, Canada, where the Great Spirit first placed the Sac nation, and inspired him with a belief that, at the end of four years, he should see a white man, who would be to him a father. Consequently he blackened his face and ate but once a day, just as the sun was going down, for three years, and continued dreaming throughout all this time, whenever he slept. The Great Spirit again appeared to him and told him that, at the end of one year more, he should meet his father, and directed him to start seven days before its expiration, and take with him his two brothers, Na-mah, or Sturgeon, and Pauk-a-hum-ma-wa, or Sunfish, and travel in a direction to the left of sun-rising. After pursuing this course for five days, he sent out his two brothers to listen if they could hear a noise, and if so, to fasten some grass to the end of a pole, erect it, pointing in the direction of the sound, and then return to him.

Early next morning they returned, and reported that they had heard sounds which appeared near at hand, and that they had fulfilled his order. They all then started for the place where the pole had been erected. On reaching it, Nanamakee left his party and went alone to the place from

13

whence the sounds proceeded, and found that the white man had arrived (2) and pitched his tent. When he came in sight, his father came out to meet him. He took him by the hand and welcomed him into his tent. He told him that he was the son of the king of France (3) ; that he had been dreaming for four years; that the Great Spirit had directed him to come here, where he should meet a nation of people who had never yet seen a white man; that they should be his children and he should be their father; that he had communicated these things to the king, his father, who laughed at him and called him Mashena, but he insisted on coming here to meet his children where the Great Spirit had directed him. The king had told him that he would find neither land nor people; that this was an uninhabited region of lakes and mountains; but finding that he would have no peace without it, he fitted out a nap-e-qua, manned it, and gave him charge of it. He had immediately loaded it, set sail, and had now landed on the very day that the Great Spirit had told him he should meet his children. He had now met the man who should, in future, have charge of all the nation.

He then presented him with a medal which he hung around his neck. Nan-a-ma-kee informed him of his dreaming, and told him that his two brothers remained a little way behind. His father gave him a shirt, a blanket, and a handkerchief besides a variety of other presents, and told him to go and bring his brethren. Having laid aside his buffalo robe and dressed himself in his new dress, he started to meet his brothers. When they met, he explained to them his meeting with the white man and exhibited the presents that he had made him. He then took off his medal and placed it on his elder brother, Na-mah, and requested them both to go with him to his father.

They proceeded thither, were ushered into the tent, and after some brief ceremony his father opened a chest and took presents therefrom for the newcomers. He discovered that Nan-a-ma-kee had given his medal to his elder brother, Na-mah. He told him that he had done wrong; that he should wear that medal himself, as he had others for his brothers. That which he had given him was typical of the rank he should hold in the nation; that his brothers could rank only as civil chiefs, and that their duties should consist in taking care of the village and attending to its civil concerns, whilst his rank, from his superior knowledge, placed him over all. If the nation should get into any difficulty with another, then his puc-co-ha-wam-a, or sovereign decree, must be obeyed. If he declared war, he must lead them on to battle; that the Great Spirit had made him a great and brave general, and had sent him here to give him that medal and make presents to him for his people.

His father remained four days, during which time he gave him guns, powder, lead, spears, and lances, and taught him their use, so that in war he might be able to chastise his enemies, and in peace, they could kill buffalo, deer and other game necessary for the comforts and luxuries of life. He then presented the others with various kinds of cooking utensils and taught them their uses. After having given them large quantities of goods as presents, and everything necessary for their comfort, he set sail for France, promising to meet them again, at the same place, after the 12th moon.

The three newly made chiefs returned to their village and explained to Muk-a-ta-quet, their father, who was the principal chief of the nation, what had been said and done.

The old chief had some dogs killed and made a feast preparatory to resigning his scepter, to which all the nation were invited. Great anxiety prevailed among them to know what the three brothers had seen and heard. The old chief arose and related the sayings and doing of his three sons, and concluded by saying that the Great Spirit had directed that these, his three sons, should take the rank and power that had once been his, and that he yielded these honors and duties willingly to them, because it was the wish of the Great Spirit, and he could never consent to make him angry. He now presented the great medicine bag to Nan-a-ma-kee, and told him that he cheerfully resigned it to him. "It is the soul of our nation; it has never yet been disgraced, and I will expect you to keep it unsullied."

Some dissensions arose among them in consequence of so much power being given to Nan-a-ma-kee, he being so young a man. To quiet them, Nan-a-ma-kee, during a violent thunderstorm, told them that he had caused it, and that it was an exemplification of the name the Great Spirit had given him. During the storm, the lightning struck and set fire to a tree near by, a sight they had never witnessed before. He went to it and brought away some of its burning branches, made a fire in the lodge, and seated his brothers around it opposite to one another, while he stood up and addressed his people as follows:

"I am yet young, but the Great Spirit has called me to the rank I hold among you. I have never sought to be more than my birth entitled me to. I have not been ambitious, nor was it ever my wish while my father was yet among the living to take his place, nor have I now usurped his powers. The Great Spirit caused me to dream for four years. He told me where to go and meet the white man who would be a kind father to us all. I obeyed. I went, and have seen and know our new father. You have all heard what was said and done. The Great Spirit directed him to come and meet me, and it is his order that places me at the head of my nation, the place which my father has willingly resigned.

"You have all witnessed the power that has been given me by the Great Spirit, in making that fire; and all that I now ask is, that these my two chiefs, may never let it go out, and that they may preserve peace among you and administer to the wants of the needy. Should an enemy invade our country, I will then, and not until then, assume command, and go forth with my band of brave warriors and endeavor to chastise them."

At the conclusion of this speech every voice cried out for Nan-a-ma-kee. All were satisfied when they found that the Great Spirit had done what they had suspected was the work of Nan-a-ma-kee, he being a very shrewd young man.

The next spring, according to promise, their French father returned, with his nap-e-qua richly laden with goods, which were distributed among them. He continued for a long time to keep up a regular trade with them, they giving him in exchange for his goods their furs and peltries.

"A FAVORABLE REPORT OF THE COUNTRY."
Looking South from the Watch Tower.

CHAPTER II.

THE SACS LEAVE CANADA—THEIR ENEMIES PURSUE THEM—ALLIANCE WITH THE FOXES—ARRIVAL AT SAUK-E-NAUK—BLACK HAWK BECOMES A BRAVE—MANY ADVENTURES.

After a long time the British overpowered the French (4), the two nations being at war, and drove them away from Quebec, taking possession of it themselves. The different tribes of Indians around our nation, envying our people, united their forces against them and by their combined strength succeeded in driving them to Montreal, and from there to Mackinac. Here our people first met our British father, who furnished them with goods. Their enemies still wantonly pursued them and drove them to different places along the lake (5). At last they made a village near Green Bay, on what is now called Sac River. Here they held a council with the Foxes, and a national treaty of friendship and alliance was agreed upon. The Foxes abandoned their village and joined the Sacs (6). This arrangement being mutually obligatory upon both parties, as neither was sufficiently strong to meet their enemies with any hope of success, they soon became as one band or nation of people. They were driven, however, by the combined forces of their enemies to the Wisconsin. They remained here for some time, until a party of their young men, who descended Rock River to its mouth, had returned and made a favorable report of the country. They all descended Rock River (7), drove the Kaskaskias from the country, and commenced the erection of their village, determined never to leave it.

BLACK HAWK'S AUTOBIOGRAPHY

At this village I was born, being a lineal descendant of the first chief, Nan-a-ma-kee, or Thunder. Few, if any, events of note occurred within my recollection until about my fifteenth year. I was not allowed to paint or wear feathers, but distinguished myself at an early age by wounding an enemy; consequently I was placed in the ranks of the braves.

Soon after this a leading chief of the Muscow nation came to our village for recruits to go to war against the Osages, our common enemy. I volunteered my services to go, as my father had joined him, and was proud to have an opportunity to prove to him that I was not an unworthy son, and that I had courage and bravery. It was not long before we met the enemy, and a battle ensued. Standing by my father's side, I saw him kill his antagonist and tear the scalp from his head. Fired with valor and ambition, I rushed furiously upon another and smote him to the earth with my tomahawk. I then run my lance through his body, took off his scalp, and returned in triumph to my father. He said nothing, but looked well pleased. This was the first man I killed. The enemy's loss in this engagement having been very great, they immediately retreated, which put an end to the war for the time being. Our party then returned to the village and danced over the scalps we had taken. This was the first time I was permitted to join in a scalp dance.

After a few moons had passed, having acquired considerable reputation as a brave, I led a party of seven and attacked one hundred Osages. I killed one man and left him for my comrades to scalp while I was taking observations of the strength and preparations of the enemy. Finding that they were equally well armed with ourselves, I ordered a retreat and came off without the loss of a man. This excursion gained for me great applause, and enabled me, before a great while, to raise a party of one hundred and eighty to march against the Osages. We left our village in high spirits and marched over a rugged country until we reached the land of the Osages on the borders of the Missouri.

We followed their trail until we arrived at the village, which we approached with exceeding caution, thinking that they were all here, but found to our sorrow that they had all deserted it. The party became dissatisfied on account of this disappointment, and all, with the exception of five noble braves, dispersed and went home. I then placed myself at the head of this brave little band, and thanked the Great Spirit that so many had remained. We took to the trail of our enemies, with a full determination never to return without some trophy of a victory. We followed cautiously on for several days, killed one man and a boy, and returned home with their scalps.

In consequence of this mutiny, I was not again able to raise a sufficient force to go against the Osages until about my nineteenth year. During this interim they committed many outrages on our nation; hence I succeeded in recruiting two hundred efficient warriors, and early one morning took up the line of march. In a few days we were in the enemy's country, and we had not gone far before we met a force equal to our own with which to contend. A general battle immediately commenced, although my warriors were considerably fatigued by forced marches. Each party fought desperately. The enemy seemed unwilling to yield the ground, and we were determined to conquer or die. A great number of Osages were killed and many wounded before they commenced a retreat. A band of warriors more brave, skillful, and efficient than mine could not be found. In this engagement I killed five men and one squaw, and had the good fortune to take the scalps of all I struck with one exception, that of the squaw, who was accidentally killed. The enemy's loss in

BLACK HAWK'S AUTOBIOGRAPHY 21

this engagement was about one hundred braves. Ours, nineteen. We then returned to our village well pleased with our success, and danced over the scalps we had taken.

In consequence of their great loss in this battle, the Osages became satisfied to remain on their own lands. This stopped for a while their depredations on our nation.

Our attention was now directed toward an ancient enemy who had decoyed and murdered some of our helpless women and children. I started with my father, who took command of a small party, and proceeded against the enemy to chastise them for the wrongs they had heaped upon us. We met near the Merrimac (8) and an action ensued; the Cherokees having a great advantage in point of numbers. Early in the engagement my father was wounded in the thigh, but succeeded in killing his enemy before he fell. Seeing that he had fallen, I assumed command, and fought desperately until the enemy commenced retreating before the well directed blows of our braves. I returned to my father to administer to his necessities, but nothing could be done for him. The medicine man said the wound was mortal, and it soon proved to be so. In this battle I killed three men and wounded several. The enemy's loss was twenty-eight and ours seven. I now fell heir to the great medicine bag of my forefathers, which had belonged to my father. I took it, buried our dead, and returned with my party to our village, sad and sorrowful, in consequence of the loss of my father. Owing to this misfortune I blackened my face, fasted and prayed to the Great Spirit for five years, during which time I remained in a civil capacity, hunting and fishing.

The Osages having again commenced aggressions on our people, and the Great Spirit having taken pity on me, I took a small party and went against them. I could find only six of them, and their forces being so weak, I thought it would be cowardly to kill them, I took them prisoners and carried them to our Spanish father at St. Louis, gave them up to him, and then returned to our village. But determined on the complete and final extermination of the dastardly Osages, in punishment for the injuries our people had received from them, I commenced recruiting a strong force, immediately on my return, and started, in the third moon, with five hundred Sacs and Foxes, and one hundred Iowas, and marched against the enemy. We continued our march for many days before we came upon their trail, which was discovered late in the day. We encamped for the night, made an early start next morning, and before sundown we fell upon forty lodges, killed all the inhabitants except two squaws, whom I took as prisoners. During this engagement I killed seven men and two boys with my own hands. In this battle many of the bravest warriors among the Osages were killed, which caused those who yet remained of their nation to keep within the boundaries of their own land and cease their aggressions upon our hunting grounds.

The loss of my father by the Cherokees made me anxious to avenge his death by the utter annihilation, if possible, of the last remnant of their tribe. I accordingly commenced collecting another party to go against them. Having succeeded in this I started with my braves and went into their country; but I found only five of their people, whom I took prisoners. I afterwards released four of them; the other, a young squaw, we brought home. Great as was my hatred of these people, I could not kill so small a party.

About the close of the ninth moon, I led a large party against the Chippewas, Kaskaskias, and Osages. This was the commencement of a long and arduous campaign, which terminated in my thirty-fifth year, after having had seven regular engagements and numerous small skirmishes. During this campaign several hundred of the enemy were slain.

I killed thirteen of their bravest warriors with my own hands.

Our enemies having now been driven from our hunting grounds, we returned in peace to our village. After the seasons of mourning and burying our dead braves and of feasting and dancing had passed, we commenced preparations for our winter's hunt. When all was ready, we started on the chase, and returned richly rewarded for our toil.

CHAPTER III.

LOUISIANA PURCHASE—HOW THE INDIANS REGARDED IT—PIKE'S VISIT—COVERING THE BLOOD—CESSION OF 1804—THE BEGINNING OF TROUBLE—BUILDING OF FORT MADISON.

We usually paid a visit to St. Louis every summer, but in consequence of the long protracted war in which we had been engaged, I had not been there for some years. Our difficulties having been all settled, I concluded to take a small party and go down to see our Spanish father during the summer. We went, and on our arrival put up our lodges where the market house now stands. After painting and dressing, we called to see our Spanish father and were kindly received. He gave us a great variety of presents and an abundance of provisions. We danced through the town as usual, and the inhabitants all seemed well pleased. They seemed to us like brothers, and always gave us good advice.

On my next and last visit to our Spanish father, I discovered on landing that all was not right. Every countenance seemed sad and gloomy. I inquired the cause, and was informed that the Americans were coming to take possession of the town and country, and that we were to lose our Spanish father. This news made me and my band exceedingly sad, because we had always heard bad accounts of the Americans from those who had lived near them. We were very sorry to lose our Spanish father, who had always treated us with great friendship. A few days afterwards, the Americans arrived. I, in company with my band, went to take leave for the last time of our father. The Americans came to see him also. Seeing their approach, we passed out at one door as they came in at another. We immedi-

BLACK HAWK'S AUTOBIOGRAPHY 25

ately embarked in our canoes for our village on Rock River, not liking the change any more than our friends at St. Louis appeared to. On arriving at our village we gave out the news that a strange people had taken possession of St. Louis, and that we should never see our generous Spanish father again. This information cast a deep gloom over our people.

Some time afterwards a boat came up the river with a young American chief, at that time Lieutenant, and afterwards General, Pike, and a small party of soldiers aboard (9). The boat at length arrived at Rock River, and the young chief came on shore with his interpreter. He made us a speech and gave us some presents, in return for which we gave him meat and such other provisions as we could spare. We were well pleased with the speech of the young chief. He gave us good advice, and said our American father would treat us well. He presented us an American flag which we hoisted. He then requested us to lower the British colors and give him our British medals, promising to send us others on his return to St. Louis. This we declined to do as we wished to have two fathers.

When the young chief started we sent runners to the village of the Foxes, some miles distant, to direct them to treat him well as he passed, which they did. He went to the head of the Mississippi and then returned to St. Louis. We did not see any Americans again for some time, being supplied with goods by British traders. We were fortunate in not giving up our medals, for we learned afterwards from our traders, that the chiefs high up the Mississippi, who gave theirs, never received any in exchange for them. But the fault was not with the young American chief. He was a good man, a great brave, and I have since learned, died in his country's service.

Some moons after this (10) young chief had descended the Mississippi, one of our people killed an American, was taken prisoner and was confined in the prison at St. Louis for the offense. We held a council at our village to see what could be done for him, and determined that Quash-qua-me, Pash-e-pa-ho, Ouch-e-qua-ka, and Hash-equar-hi-qua should go down to St. Louis, see our American father, and do all they could to have our friend released by paying for the person killed, thus covering the blood and satisfying the relations of the murdered man. This being the only means with us for saving a person who had killed another, we then thought it was the same way with the whites.

The party started with the good wishes of the whole nation, who had high hopes that the emissaries would accomplish the object of their mission. The relations of the prisoner blackened their faces and fasted, hoping the Great Spirit would take pity on them and return husband and father to his sorrowing wife and weeping children.

Quash-qua-me and party remained a long time absent. They at length returned and encamped near the village, a short distance below it, and did not come up that day, nor did any one approach their camp. They appeared to be dressed in fine coats and had medals. From these circumstances we were in hopes that they had brought good news. Early the next morning the council lodge was crowded; Quash-qua-me and party came up and gave us the following account of their mission:

"On our arrival at St. Louis we met our American father and explained to him our business, urging the release of our friend. The American chief told us he wanted land. We agreed to give him some on the west side of the Mississippi, likewise more on the Illinois side opposite Jeffreon (now called North Fabius River, in Missouri). When the business was all arranged we expected to have our friend released to come home with us. About the time we were ready to start, our brother was let out of the prison. He started and ran a short distance when he was shot dead."

This was all they could remember of what had been said and done. It subsequently appeared that they had been drunk the greater part of the time while at St. Louis.

This was all myself and nation knew of the treaty of 1804. It has since been explained to me. I found by that treaty, that all of the country east of the Mississippi and south of Jeffreon was ceded to the United States for one thousand dollars a year. I will leave it to the people of the United States to say whether our nation was properly represented in that treaty; or whether we received a fair compensation for the extent of country ceded by these four individuals (11). I could say much more respecting this treaty, but I will not at this time. It has been the origin of all our serious difficulties with the whites (12).

Some time after this treaty was made, a war chief with a party of soldiers came up the river in keel boats, encamped a short distance above the head of the Des Moines Rapids, and commenced cutting timber and building houses. The news of their arrival was soon carried to all our villages, to confer upon which many councils were held. We could not understand the intention or comprehend the reason why the Americans wanted to build houses at that place. We were told that they were a party of soldiers, who had brought great guns with them, and looked like a war party of whites.

A number of people immediately went down to see what was going on, myself among them. On our arrival we found that they were building a fort (13). The soldiers were busily engaged in cutting timber, and I observed that they took their guns with them when they went to the woods. The whole party acted as they would do in an enemy's country. The chiefs held a council with the officers, or head men of the party, which I did not attend, but understood from them that the war chief had said that they were building houses for a trader who was coming there to live, and would sell us goods very cheap, and that the soldiers were to remain to keep him company. We were pleased at this information and hoped that it was all true; but we were not so credulous as to believe that all these buildings were intended merely for the accommodation of a trader. Being distrustful of their intentions, we were anxious for them to leave off building and go back down the river.

By this time a considerable number of Indians had arrived to see what was doing. I discovered that the whites were alarmed. Some of our young men watched a party of soldiers who went out to work carrying their arms, which were laid aside before they commenced. Having stolen quietly to the spot, they seized the guns and gave a wild yell. The party threw down their axes and ran for their arms, but found them gone and themselves surrounded. Our young men laughed at them and returned their weapons.

When this party came to the fort they reported what had been done, and the war chief made a serious affair of it. He called our chiefs to council inside of his fort. This created considerable excitement in our camp, every one wanting to know what was going to be done. The picketing which had been put up, being low, every Indian crowded around the fort, got upon blocks of wood and old barrels that they might see what was going on inside. Some were armed with guns and others with bows and arrows. We used this precaution, seeing that the soldiers had their guns loaded, and having seen them load their big guns in the morning.

A party of our braves commenced dancing and proceeded up to the gate with the intention of going in, but were stopped. The council immediately broke up; the soldiers with their guns in their hands rushed out from the rooms where they had been concealed. The cannon were hauled to the gateway, and a soldier came running with fire in his hand, ready to apply the match. Our braves gave way and retired to the camp. There was no preconcerted plan to attack the whites at that time, but I am of the opinion now that had our braves got into the fort, all of the whites would have been killed, as were the British soldiers at Mackinac many years before (14).

We broke up our camp and returned to Rock River. A short time afterwards the party at the fort received reinforcements, among whom we observed some of our old friends from St. Louis.

Soon after our return from Fort Madison runners came to our village from the Shawnee prophet (15). Others were dispatched by him to the village of the Winnebagoes, with invitations to meet him on the Wabash. Accordingly a party went from each village. All of our party returned, among whom came a prophet, who explained to us the bad treatment the different nations of Indians had received from the Americans, by giving them a few presents and taking their lands from them.

I remember well his saying: "If you do not join your friends on the Wabash, the Americans will take this very village from you." I little thought then that his words would come true, supposing that he used these arguments merely to encourage us to join him, which we concluded not to do. He then returned to the Wabash, where a party of Winnebagoes had preceded, and preparations were making for war. A battle soon ensued [probably the battle of Tippecanoe] in which several Winnebagoes were killed. As soon as their nation heard of this battle, and that some of their people had been killed, they sent several war parties in different directions: one to the mining country, one to Prairie du Chien, and another to Fort Madison. The latter returned by way of our village and exhibited several scalps which they had taken. Their success induced several parties to go against the fort. Myself and several of my band joined the last party (16), and we were determined to take the fort. We arrived in the vicinity during the night. The spies that we had sent out several days before to watch the movements of those at the garrison, and ascertain their numbers, came to us and gave the following information: "A keel arrived from below this evening with seventeen men. There are about fifty men in the fort and they march out every morning to exercise." It was immediately determined that we should conceal ourselves in a position as near as practicable to where the soldiers should come out, and when the signal was given, each one was to fire on them and rush into the fort. With my knife I dug a hole in the ground deep enough that by placing a few weeds around it I could conceal myself. I was so near the fort that I could hear the sentries walking on their beats. By daybreak I had finished my work and was anxiously awaiting the rising of the sun. The morning drum beat. I examined the priming of my gun, and eagerly watched for the gate to open. It did open, but instead of the troops, a young man came out alone and the gate closed after him. He passed so close to me that I could have killed him with my knife, but I let him pass unharmed. He kept the path toward the river, and had he gone one step from it, he must have come upon us and would have been killed. He returned immediately and entered the gate. I would now have rushed for the gate and entered it with him, but I feared that our party was not prepared to follow me.

The gate opened again when four men emerged and went down to the river for wood. While they were gone, another man came out, walked toward the river, was fired on, and killed by a Winnebago. The others started and ran rapidly towards the fort, but two of them were shot dead. We then took shelter under the river's bank out of reach of the firing from the fort. The firing now commenced from both parties and was kept up without cessation all day. I advised our party to set fire to the fort, and commenced preparing arrows for that purpose. At night we made the attempt, and succeeded in firing the building several times, but without effect, as it was always extinguished.

The next day I took my rifle and shot in two the cord by which they hoisted their flag, and prevented them from raising it again. We continued firing until our ammunition was expended. Finding that we could not take the fort, we returned home, having one Winnebago killed and one wounded during the siege.

I have since learned that the trader who lived in the fort wounded the Winnebago while he was scalping the first man that was killed. The Winnebago recovered, and is now living, and is very friendly disposed towards the trader, believing him to be a great brave.

CHAPTER IV.

WAR OF 1812—EXECUTION OF AN INDIAN—SACS OFFER
THEIR SERVICES TO THE AMERICANS—MADISON DIRECTS
THEM TO REMAIN NEUTRAL—WHY THE SACS JOINED
THE BRITISH ARMY—FORTS MEIGS AND STEPHENSON—
A CHAPTER OF ADVENTURES.

Soon after our return home, news reached us that a war was going to take place between the British and the Americans. Runners continued to arrive from different tribes, all confirming the reports of the expected war. The British agent, Colonel Dixon, was holding talks with and making presents to the different tribes. I had not made up my mind whether to join the British or remain neutral. I had not discovered yet one good trait in the character of the Americans who had come to the country. They made fair promises, but never fulfilled them, while the British made but few, and we could always rely on their word.

One of our people having killed a Frenchman at Prairie du Chien, the British took him prisoner and said they would shoot him next day. His family were encamped a short distance below the mouth of the Wisconsin. He begged permission to go and see them that night, as he was to die the next day. They permitted him to go after he had promised to return by sunrise the next morning. He visited his family, which consisted of his wife and six children. I cannot describe their meeting and parting so as to be understood by the whites, as it appears that their feelings are acted upon by certain rules laid down by their preachers, while ours are governed by the monitor within us. He bade his loved ones the last sad farewell and hurried across the prairie to the fort and arrived in time. The

BLACK HAWK'S AUTOBIOGRAPHY   33

soldiers were ready and immediately marched out and shot him down. I visited the stricken family, and by hunting and fishing provided for them until they reached their relations.

Why did the Great Spirit ever send the whites to this land to drive us from our homes and introduce among us poisonous liquors, disease, and death? They should have remained in the land the Great Spirit allotted them. But I will proceed with my story. My memory, however, is not very good since my late visit to the white people. I have still a buzzing noise in my ears from the noise and bustle incident to travel. I may give some parts of my story out of place, but will make my best endeavors to be correct.

Several of our chiefs were called upon to go to Washington to see our great father (President Madison). They started, and during their absence I went to Peoria, on the Illinois River, to see my old friend (Thomas Forsythe, the trader) and get his advice. He was a man who always told us the truth, and knew everything that was going on. When I arrived at Peoria he had gone to Chicago, and was not at home. I visited the Pottawattomie villages and then returned to Rock River. Soon after this, our friends returned from their visit to the great father and reported what had been said and done. The great father told them that in the event of a war taking place with England, not to interfere on either side, but to remain neutral. He did not want our help, but wished us to hunt and supply our families, and remain at peace. He said that British traders would not be allowed to come on the Mississippi to furnish goods, but that we would be well supplied by an American trader. Our chiefs then told him that the British traders always gave us credit in the fall for guns, powder, and goods, to enable us to hunt and clothe our families. He replied that the trader at Fort Madison would have plenty of goods, and if we should go there in the autumn, he would supply us on credit, as the British traders had done. The party gave a good account of what they had seen and the kind treatment they had received. This information pleased us all very much. We all agreed to follow our great father's advice and not interfere in the war. Our women were much pleased at the good news. Everything went on cheerfully in our village. We resumed our pastimes (17) of playing ball, horse racing, and dancing, which had been laid aside when this great war was first talked about. We had fine crops of corn which were now ripe, and our women were busily engaged in gathering it and making caches to contain it. (See note 28.)

In a short time we were ready to start to Fort Madison to get our supply of goods, that we might proceed to our hunting grounds. We passed merrily down the river, all in high spirits. I had determined to spend the winter at my old favorite hunting grounds on Skunk River. I left part of my corn and mats at its mouth to take up as we returned, and many others did the same.

The next morning we arrived at the fort and made our encampment. Myself and principal men paid a visit to the war chief at the fort. He received us kindly, and gave us some tobacco, pipes, and provisions. The trader came in and we all shook hands with him, for on him all our dependence was placed, to enable us to hunt and thereby support our families. We waited a long time, expecting the trader would tell us that he had orders from our great father to supply us with goods, but he said nothing on the subject. I got up and told him in a short speech what we had come for, and hoped he had plenty of goods to supply us. I told him he should be well paid in the spring, and concluded by informing him that we had decided to follow our great father's advice and not go to war.

He said that he was happy to hear that we had concluded to remain at peace. He said that he had a large quantity of goods, and that if we made a good hunt we should be well supplied; but he remarked that he had no instructions to furnish us anything on credit, nor could he give us any without receiving the pay for them.

We told him what our great father had said to our chiefs at Washington, and contended that he could supply us if he would, believing that our great father always spoke the truth. The war chief said the trader could not furnish us on credit, and that he had received no such instructions from our great father at Washington.

We left the fort dissatisfied and went to camp. What was now to be done, we knew not. We questioned the party that brought us the news from our great father, that we could get credit for our winter supplies at this place. They still told us the same story and insisted on its truth. Few of us slept that night. All was gloom and discontent.

In the morning a canoe was seen descending the river, bearing an express, who brought intelligence that La Gutrie, a British trader, had landed at Rock Island with two boat-loads of goods. He requested us to come up immediately as he had good news for us, and a variety of presents. The express presented us with tobacco, pipes, and wampum. The news ran through our camp like fire through dry grass on the prairie. Our lodges were soon taken down and we all started for Rock Island. Here ended all hopes of our remaining at peace. We had been forced into war by being deceived.

Our party were not long in getting to Rock Island. When we came in sight and saw tents pitched, we yelled, fired our guns, and beat our drums. Guns at the island were immediately fired, returning our salute, and a British flag hoisted. We landed, were cordially received by La Gutrie, and then smoked the pipe with him, after which he made a speech to us saying that he had been sent by Colonel Dixon. [This Colonel Dixon had long been a British trader among the Indians, and at the beginning of the war of 1812 had given his services to the British.] He gave us a number of handsome presents, among them a large silk flag and a keg of rum. He then told us to retire, take some refreshments and rest ourselves, as he would have more to say to us next day.

We accordingly retired to our lodges, which in the meantime had been put up, and spent the night. The next morning we called upon him and told him we wanted his two boat loads of goods to divide among our people, for which he should be well paid in the spring in furs and peltries. He consented that we should take them and do as we pleased with them. While our people were dividing the goods, he took me aside and informed me that Colonel Dixon was at Green Bay with twelve boats loaded with goods, guns, and ammunition. He wished to raise a party immediately and go to him. He said our friend, the trader at Peoria, was collecting the Pottawattomies, and would be there before us. I communicated this information to my braves, and a party of two hundred warriors were soon collected and ready to depart. I paid a visit to the lodge of an old friend, who had been the comrade of my youth, and had been in many war parties with me, but was now crippled and no longer able to travel. He had a son whom I had adopted as my own, and who had hunted with me the two winters preceding. I wished my old friend to let him go with me. He objected, saying he could not get his support if he did attend me, and that I, who had always provided for him since his misfortune, would be gone; therefore, having no other dependence, he could not spare him. I offered to leave my son in his stead but he refused to give his consent. He said that he did not like the war, as he had been down the river and had been well treated by the Americans and could not fight against them. He had promised to winter near a white settler above Salt River, and must take his son with him. We parted and I soon completed my arrangements and started with my party for Green Bay. On our arrival there we found a large encampment; were well received by Colonel Dixon and the war chiefs who were with him. He gave us plenty of provisions, tobacco, and pipes, saying that he would hold a council with us the next day. In the encampment I found a great number of Kickapoos, Ottawas, and Winnebagoes. I visited all their camps, and found them in high spirits. They had all received new guns, ammunition, and a variety of clothing.

In the evening a messenger came to visit Colonel Dixon. I went to his tent, in which there were two other war chiefs and an interpreter. He received me with a hearty shake of the hand; presented me to the other chiefs, who treated me cordially, expressing themselves as being much pleased to meet me. After I was seated Colonel Dixon said: "General Black Hawk, I sent for you to explain to you what we are going to do and to give you the reasons for our coming here. Our friend, La Gutrie, informs us in the letter you brought from him, of what has taken place. You will now have to hold us fast by the hand. Your English father has found out that the Americans want to take your country from you and has sent me and my braves to drive them back to their own country. He has, likewise, sent a large quantity of arms and ammunition, and we want all your warriors to join us."

He then placed a medal around my neck and gave me a paper, which I lost in the late war, and a silk flag, saying: "You are to command all the braves that will leave here the day after tomorrow, to join our braves at Detroit."

I told him I was very much disappointed, as I wanted to descend the Mississippi and make war on the settlements. He said that he had been ordered to lay in waste the country around St. Louis; but having been a trader on the Mississippi for many years himself, and always having been treated kindly by the people there, he could not send brave men to murder helpless women and innocent children. There were no soldiers there for us to fight, and where he was going to send us, there were a great many of them. If we defeated them, the Mississippi country should be ours. I was much pleased with this speech, as it was spoken by a brave.

I inquired about my old friend (Forsythe), the trader at Peoria, and said that I had expected that he would have been here before we were.

He shook his head and said: "I have sent express after express for him, and offered him great sums of money to come and bring the Pottawattomies and Kickapoos with him. He has refused, saying that the British father has not money enough to induce him to join us. But I have now laid a trap for him. I have sent Gomo and a party of Indians to take him prisoner and bring him here alive. I expect him in a few days."

The next day, arms and ammunition, knives, tomahawks, and clothing were given to my band. We had a great feast in the evening, and the morning following I started with about five hundred braves to join the British army. We passed Chicago and observed that the fort had been evacuated by the Americans, and their soldiers had gone to Fort Wayne. They were attacked a short distance from the fort and defeated (18). They had a considerable quantity of powder in the fort at Chicago, which they had promised to the Indians, but the night before they marched away they destroyed it by throwing it into a well. If they had kept their word to the Indians, they doubtless would have gone to Fort Wayne without molestation. On our arrival, I found that the Indians had several prisoners, and I advised them to threat them well.

We continued our march, joining the British below Detroit, soon after which we had a battle. The Americans fought well, and drove us back with considerable loss. I was greatly surprised at this, as I had been told that the Americans would not fight.

Our next movement was against a fortified place (19). I was stationed with my braves to prevent any person going to or coming from the fort. I found two men taking care of cattle and took them prisoners. I would not kill them, but delivered them to the British war chief. Soon afterwards, several boats came down the river full of American soldiers. They landed on the opposite side, took the British batteries, and pursued the soldiers that had left them. They went too far without knowing the strength of the British and were defeated. I hurried across the river, anxious for an opportunity to show the courage of my braves, but before we reached the scene of battle, all was over.

The British had taken many prisoners and the Indians were killing them. I immediately put a stop to it, as I never thought it brave, but base and cowardly, to kill an unarmed and helpless foe. We remained here some time. I cannot detail what took place, as I was stationed with my braves in the woods. It appeared, however, that the British could not take this fort, for we marched to another some distance off. When we approached it, I found a small stockade, and concluded that there were not many men in it. The British war chief sent a flag of truce. Colonel Dixon carried it, but soon returned, reporting that the young war chief in command (20) would not give up the fort without fighting. Colonel Dixon came to me and said, "You will see tomorrow how easily we will take that fort." I was of the same opinion, but when the morning came I was disappointed. The British advanced and commenced the attack, fighting like true braves, but were defeated by the braves in the fort, and a great number of our men were killed.

The British army was making preparations to retreat. I was now tired of being with them, our success being bad, and having got no plunder. I determined on leaving them and returning to Rock River, to see what had become of my wife and children, as I had not heard from them since I left home. That night I took about twenty of my braves, and left the British camp for home. On our journey we met no one until we came to the Illinois River. Here we found two lodges of Pottawattomies. They received us in a very friendly manner, and gave us something to eat. I inquired about their friends who were with the British. They said there had been some fighting on the Illinois River and that my friend, the Peoria trader, had been taken prisoner. "By Gomo and his party?" I immediately inquired. They replied, "No, but by the Americans, who came up with boats. They took him and the French settlers prisoners, and then burned the village." [The leader of this unwarranted attack upon a loyal community was Capt. Thomas E. Craig, who was shot at the battle of the Sinkhole by Black Hawk. The incident above narrated occurred Nov. 8, 1812. See note 22.—ED.] They could give us no information regarding our friends on Rock River. In three days more, we were in the vicinity of our village, and were soon afterwards surprised to find that a party of Americans had followed us from the British camp. One of them, more daring than his comrades, had made his way through the thicket on foot, and was just in the act of shooting me, when I discovered him. I then ordered him to surrender, marched him into camp, and turned him over to a number of our young men with this injunction: "Treat him as a brother, as I have concluded to adopt him as one of our tribe" (21).

A little while before this occurrence I had directed my party to proceed to the village, as I had discovered a smoke ascending from a hollow in the bluff, and wished to go alone to the spot from which the smoke proceeded, to see who was there. I approached the spot, and when I came in view of the fire, I saw an old man sitting in sorrow beneath a mat which he had stretched over him. At any other time I would have turned away without disturbing him, knowing that he came here to be alone, to humble himself before the Great Spirit, that he might take pity on him. I approached and seated myself beside him. He gave one look at me, and then fixed his eyes on the ground. It was my old friend. I anxiously inquired for his son, my adopted child, and what had befallen our people. My old comrade seemed scarcely alive. He must have fasted a long time. I lighted my pipe and put it into his mouth. He eagerly drew a few puffs, cast up his eyes which met mine, and recognized me. His eyes were glassy and he would have fallen into forgetfulness, had I not given him some water, which revived him. I again inquired what had become of our son, and what had befallen our people.

In a feeble voice he said: "Soon after your departure to join the British, I descended the river with a small party, to winter at the place I told you the white man had asked me to come. When we arrived I found that a fort had been built, and the white family that had invited me to come and hunt near them had removed to it. I then paid a visit to the fort to tell the white people that my little band were friendly, and that we wished to hunt in the vicinity of the fort. The war chief who commanded there, told me we might hunt on the Illinois side of the Mississippi, and no person would trouble us; that the horsemen ranged on the Missouri side only, and that he had directed them not to cross the river. I was pleased with this assurance of safety, and immediately crossed over, and made my winter's camp. Game was plenty. We lived happy, and often talked of you. My boy regretted your absence and the hardships you would have to undergo. We had been here about two moons, when my boy went out as usual to hunt. Night came on and he did not return. I was alarmed for his safety and passed a sleepless night. In the morning my old woman went to the other lodges and gave the alarm, and all turned out to hunt for the missing one. There being snow upon the ground they soon came upon his tracks, and after pursuing it for some distance, found he was on the trail of a deer, which led toward the river. They soon came to the place where he had stood and fired, and near by, hanging on the branch of a tree, found the deer, which he had killed and skinned. But here were also found the tracks of white men. They had taken my boy prisoner. Their tracks led across the river and then down towards the fort. My friends followed on the trail, and soon found my boy lying dead. He had been most cruelly murdered. His face was shot to pieces, his body stabbed in several places and his head scalped. His arms were pinioned behind him."

The old man paused for some time, and then told me that his wife had died on their way up the Mississippi. I took the hand of my old friend in mine and pledged myself to avenge the death of his son. It was now dark, and a terrible storm was raging. The rain was descending in heavy torrents, the thunder was rolling in the heavens, and the lightning flashed across the sky. I had taken my blanket off and wrapped it around the feeble old man. When the storm abated I kindled a fire and took hold of my old friend to remove him nearer to it. He was dead. I remained with him during the night. Some of my party came early in the morning to look for me, and assisted me in burying him on the peak of the bluff. I then returned to the village with my friends. I visited the grave of my old friend as I ascended Rock River the last time.

CHAPTER V.

BLACK HAWK'S OPINION OF BRITISH AND AMERICAN MODES OF FIGHTING—HOW KEOKUK WAS MADE CHIEF—HE AVENGES THE DEATH OF HIS ADOPTED SON—BATTLE AT FORT HOWARD—DEATH OF WASH-E-OWN.

On my arrival at the village I was met by the chiefs and braves and was conducted to the lodge which was prepared for me. After eating I gave a full account of all that I had seen and done. I explained to my people the manner in which the British and Americans fought. Instead of stealing upon each other and taking every advantage to kill the enemy and save their own people as we do, which with us is considered good policy in a war chief, they march out in open daylight and fight regardless of the number of warriors they may lose. After the battle is over, they retire to feast and drink wine as if nothing had happened. After which they make a statement in writing of what they have done, each party claiming the victory, and neither giving an account of half the number killed on their side. They all fought like braves, but would not do to lead a party with us. Our maxim is, kill the enemy and save our own men. Those chiefs will do to paddle a canoe but not to steer it. The Americans shot better than the British, but their soldiers were not so well clothed nor so well provided for.

The village chief informed me that after I started with my braves and the parties who followed, the nation was reduced to a small party of fighting men; that they would have been unable to defend themselves if the Americans had attacked them. That all the women and children and old men belonging to the warriors who had joined the British were left with them to provide for. A council had been called which agreed that Quash-qua-me, the Lance, and other chiefs, with the old men, women and children, and such others as chose to accompany them, should descend the Mississippi to St. Louis, and place themselves under the American chief stationed there. They accordingly went down to St. Louis, were received as the friendly band of our nation, were sent up the Missouri, and provided for, while their friends were assisting the British. Keokuk was then introduced to me as the war chief of the braves then in the village. I inquired how he had become chief. They said that a large armed force was seen by their spies going toward Peoria. Fears were entertained that they would come up and attack the village, and a council had been called to decide as to the best course to be adopted, which concluded upon leaving the village and going to the west side of the Mississippi to get out of the way. Keokuk, during the sitting of the council, had been standing at the door of the lodge, not being allowed to enter, as he had never killed an enemy, where he remained until old Wacome came out. He then told him that he had heard what they had decided on, and was anxious to be permitted to speak before the council adjourned. Wacome returned and asked leave for Keokuk to come in and make a speech. His request was granted. Keokuk entered and addressed the chiefs. He said: "I have heard with sorrow that you have determined to leave our village and cross the Mississippi, merely because you have been told that the Americans were coming in this direction. Would you leave our village, desert our homes, and fly before an enemy approaches? Would you leave all, even the graves of our fathers, to the mercy of an enemy without trying to defend them? Give me charge of your warriors and I will defend the village while you sleep in safety."

The council consented that Keokuk should be war chief. He marshaled his braves, sent out spies and advanced with

BLACK HAWK'S AUTOBIOGRAPHY 45

a party himself on the trail leading to Peoria. They returned without seeing an enemy. The Americans did not come by our village. All were satisfied with the appointment of Keokuk. He used every precaution that our people should not be surprised. This is the manner and the cause of his receiving the appointment. I was satisfied, and then started to visit my wife and children. I found them well, and my boys were growing finely.

It is not customary for us to say much about our women, as they generally perform their part cheerfully and never interfere with business belonging to the men. This is the only wife I ever had or ever will have. She is a good woman, and teaches my boys to be brave. Here I would have rested myself and enjoyed the comforts of my lodge, but I could not. I had promised to avenge the death of my adopted son.

I immediately collected a party of thirty braves, and explained to them the object of my making this war party, which was to avenge the death of my adopted son, who had been cruelly and wantonly murdered by the whites. I explained to them the pledge I had made to his father, and told them they were the last words he had heard spoken. All were willing to go with me to fulfill my word. We started in canoes, and descended the Mississippi until we arrived near the place where Fort Madison had stood. It had been abandoned and burned by the whites, and nothing remained but the chimneys. We were pleased to see that the white people had retired from the country. We proceeded down the river again. I landed with one brave near Cape Gray; the remainder of the party went to the mouth of the Cuivre. I hurried across to the trail that led from the mouth of the Cuivre to a fort and soon afterwards heard firing at the mouth of the Creek. Myself and brave concealed ourselves on the side of the road. We had not remained here long before two men, riding one horse, came at full speed from the direction of the sound of the firing. When they came sufficiently near we fired; the horse jumped and both fell. We rushed toward them, and one rose and ran. I followed him and was gaining on him, when he ran over a pile of rails that had lately been made, seized a stick and struck at me. I now had an opportunity to see his face and I knew him. He had been at Quashquame's village to teach his people how to plow. We looked upon him as a good man. I did not wish to kill him, and pursued him no farther. I returned and met my brave. He said he had killed the other man, and had his scalp in his hand. We had not proceeded far before we met the man supposed to be killed, coming up the road, staggering like a drunken man, and covered all over with blood. This was the most terrible sight I had ever seen. I told my comrade to kill him to put him out of his misery. I could not look at him. I passed on and heard a rustling in the bushes. I distinctly saw two little boys concealing themselves in the undergrowth, thought of my own children, and passed on without noticing them.

My comrade here joined me, and in a little while we met the other detachment of our party. I told them that we would be pursued, and directed them to follow me. We crossed the creek and formed ourselves in the timber. We had not been here long before a party of mounted men rushed at full speed upon us. I took deliberate aim and shot the leader of the party. He fell lifeless from his horse. All my people fired, but without effect. The enemy rushed upon us without giving us time to reload. They surrounded us and forced us into a deep sink-hole, at the bottom of which were some bushes (22). We reloaded our guns and awaited the approach of our enemy. They rushed to the edge of the sink-hole, fired at us, and killed one of our men. We instantly returned their fire, killing one of their party. We reloaded and commenced digging holes in the side of the bank to protect ourselves, while a party watched the enemy, expecting their whole force would be upon us immediately. Some of my warriors commenced singing their death songs. I heard the whites talking, and called upon them to come out and fight. I did not like the situation, and wished the matter settled. I soon heard chopping and knocking. I could not imagine what they were doing. Soon afterwards they ran up a battery on wheels and fired without hurting any of us. They gave up the siege and returned to their fort about dusk. There were eighteen in this trap with me. We came out unharmed, with the exception of the brave who was killed by the enemy's first fire, after we were entrapped. We found one white man dead at the edge of the sink-hole, whom they did not remove for fear of our fire, and scalped him, placing our dead brave upon him, thinking we could not leave him in a better situation than on the prostrate form of a foe.

We had now effected our purpose and concluded to go back by land, thinking it unsafe to use our canoes. I found my wife and children and the greater part of our people at the mouth of the Iowa River. I now determined to remain with my family and hunt for them, and to humble myself before the Great Spirit, returning thanks to him for preserving me through the war. I made my hunting camp on the English River, which is a branch of the Iowa.

During the winter a party of Pottawattomies came from the Illinois to pay me a visit, among whom was Wash-e-own, an old man who had formerly lived at our village. He informed us that in the fall the Americans had built a fort at Peoria, and had prevented them from going down the Sangamon to hunt. He said they were very much distressed. Gomo had returned from the British army, and brought news of their defeat near Malden. He told us that he had gone to the American chief with a flag, gave up fighting, and told him that he desired to make peace for his nation. The American chief gave him a paper to the war chief at Peoria, and I visited that fort with Gomo. It was then agreed that there should be no more hostilities between the Pottawattomies and the Americans. Two of the white chiefs, with eight Pottawattomie braves, and five others, Americans, had gone down to St. Louis to have the treaty of peace confirmed. This, said Wash-e-own, is good news; for we can now go to our hunting grounds; and for my part, I never had anything to do with the war. The Americans never killed any of our people before the war, nor interfered with our hunting grounds, and I resolved to do nothing against them. I made no reply to these remarks, as the speaker was old and talked like a child.

We gave the Pottawattomies a great feast. I presented Washeown with a good horse. My braves gave one to each of his party, and at parting, said they wished us to make peace with the whites, which we did not promise, but told them we would not send out any war parties against the settlements.

A short time after the Pottawattomies had gone, a party of thirty braves belonging to our nation, from the peace camp on the Missouri, paid us a visit. They exhibited five scalps which they had taken on the Missouri, and wished us to join in a dance over them, which we willingly did. They related the manner in which they had taken these scalps. Myself and braves showed them the two we had taken near the Cuivre, and told them the cause that induced us to go out with the war party, as well as the manner in which we had taken these scalps, and the difficulty we had in obtaining them.

They recounted to us all that had taken place, the number that had been slain by the peace party, as they were called, which far exceeded what our warriors, who had joined the British, had killed. This party came for the

BATTLE GROUND AT CAMPBELL'S ISLAND.

purpose of joining the British, but I advised them to return to the peace party, and told them the news which the Pottawattomies had brought. They returned to the Missouri, accompanied by some of my braves whose families were there.

After sugar-making was over in the spring, I visited the Fox village at the lead mines. They had had nothing to do with the war, and consequently were not in mourning. I remained there some days, spending my time very pleasantly in feasting and dancing. I then paid a visit to the Pottawattomie villages on the Illinois River, and learned that San-a-tu-wa and Tat-a-pucky had been to St. Louis. Gomo told me that peace had been made between his people and the Americans, and that seven of his band remained with the war chief to make the peace stronger. He then said: "Wash-e-own is dead. He had gone to the fort to carry some wild fowl to exchange for tobacco, pipes and other articles. He had secured some tobacco and a little flour, and left the fort before sunset, but had not proceeded far when he was shot dead by a white war chief, who had concealed himself near the path for that purpose. He then dragged him to the lake and threw him in, where I afterwards found him. I have since given two horses and a rifle to his relatives, not to break the peace, to which they have agreed."

I remained some time at the village of Gomo, and went with him to the fort to pay a visit to the war chief. I spoke the Pottawattomie tongue well, and was taken for one of their people by him. He treated us in a friendly manner, and said he was very much displeased about the murder of Washeown. He promised he would find out and punish the person who killed him. He made some inquiries about the Sacs, which I answered.

CHAPTER VI.

BATTLE AT CAMPBELL'S ISLAND—BAD MEDICINE—GENERAL TAYLOR'S REPULSE AT ROCK RIVER—A TEMPERANCE MAN'S DREAM OF SNAKES—BLACK HAWK'S PEACE RESOLUTION.

On my return to Rock River, I was informed that a party of soldiers had gone up the Mississippi to build a fort at Prairie du Chien. They stopped near our village, appearing very friendly, and were treated kindly by our people (23).

We commenced repairing our lodges, putting our village in order, and clearing our cornfields. We divided the fields belonging to the party on the Missouri among those who wanted them on condition that they should be relinquished to their owners on their return from the peace establishment. We were again happy in our village. Our women went cheerfully to work, and all moved on harmoniously.

Some time afterward, five or six boats arrived loaded with soldiers on their way to Prairie du Chien to reinforce the garrison at that place. They appeared friendly and were well received, and we held a council with the war chief. We had no intention of hurting him or any of his party, for we could easily have defeated them. They remained with us all day and gave our people plenty of whisky. During the night a British party arrived, by way of Rock River, who brought us six kegs of powder. They told us that the British had gone to Prairie du Chien and had taken the fort. They wished us again to join them in the war, which we agreed to do. I collected my warriors and determined to pursue the boats, which had sailed with a fair wind. If we had known the day before, we

BLACK HAWK'S AUTOBIOGRAPHY 51

could easily have taken them all, as the war chief used no precaution to prevent it.

I started immediately with my party, by land, in pursuit, thinking that some of their boats might get aground, or that the Great Spirit would put them in our power, if he wished them taken and their people killed. About half way up the rapids I had a full view of the boats all sailing with a strong wind. I discovered that one boat was badly managed, and was suffered to be drawn ashore by the wind (24). They landed by running hard aground and lowered their sail. The others passed on. This boat the Great Spirit gave us. All that could, hurried aboard, but they were unable to push off, being fast aground. We advanced to the river's bank under cover, and commenced firing on the boat. I encouraged my braves to continue firing. Several guns were fired back from the boat, but without effect. I prepared my bow and arrows to throw fire to the sail, which was lying on the boat. After two or three attempts, I succeeded in setting it on fire. The boat was soon in flames. About this time, one of the boats that had passed returned, dropped anchor and swung in close to one which was on fire, taking off all the people except those who were killed or badly wounded. We could distinctly see them passing from one boat to the other, and fired on them with good effect. We wounded the war chief in this way. Another boat now came down, dropped her anchor, which did not take hold, and drifted ashore. The other boat cut her cable and drifted down the river, leaving their comrades without attempting to assist them. We then commenced an attack upon this boat, firing several rounds which was not returned. We thought they were afraid or only had a few aboard. I therefore ordered a rush toward the boat, but when we got near enough they fired, killing two of our braves—these being all we lost in the engagement. Some of their men jumped out and shoved the boat off, and thus got away without losing a man. I had a good opinion of this war chief, as he managed so much better than the others. It would give me pleasure to shake him by the hand.

We now put out the fire on the captured boat to save the cargo, when a skiff was seen coming down the river. Some of our people cried out, "Here comes an express from Prairie du Chien." We hoisted the British flag, but they would not land. They turned their little boat around, and rowed up the river. We directed a few shots at them, but they were so far off that we could not hurt them. I found several barrels of whisky on the captured boat, knocked in the heads and emptied the bad medicine into the river. I next found a box full of small bottles and packages, which appeared to be bad medicine also, such as the medicine men kill the white people with when they are sick. This I threw into the river. Continuing my search for plunder, I found several guns, some large barrels filled with clothing, and a number of cloth lodges, all of which I distributed among my warriors. We now disposed of the dead, and returned to the Fox village opposite the lower end of Rock Island, where we put up our new lodges and hoisted the British flag. A great many of our braves were dressed in the uniform clothing which we had taken from the Americans, which gave our encampment the appearance of a regular camp of soldiers. We placed our sentinels and commenced dancing over the scalps we had taken. Soon afterwards several boats passed down, among them a very large one carrying big guns. Our young men followed them some distance, but could do them no damage more than to scare them. We were now certain that the fort at Prairie du Chien had been taken, as this large boat went up with the first party who built the fort.

In the course of the day some of the British came down in a small boat. They had followed the large one, thinking

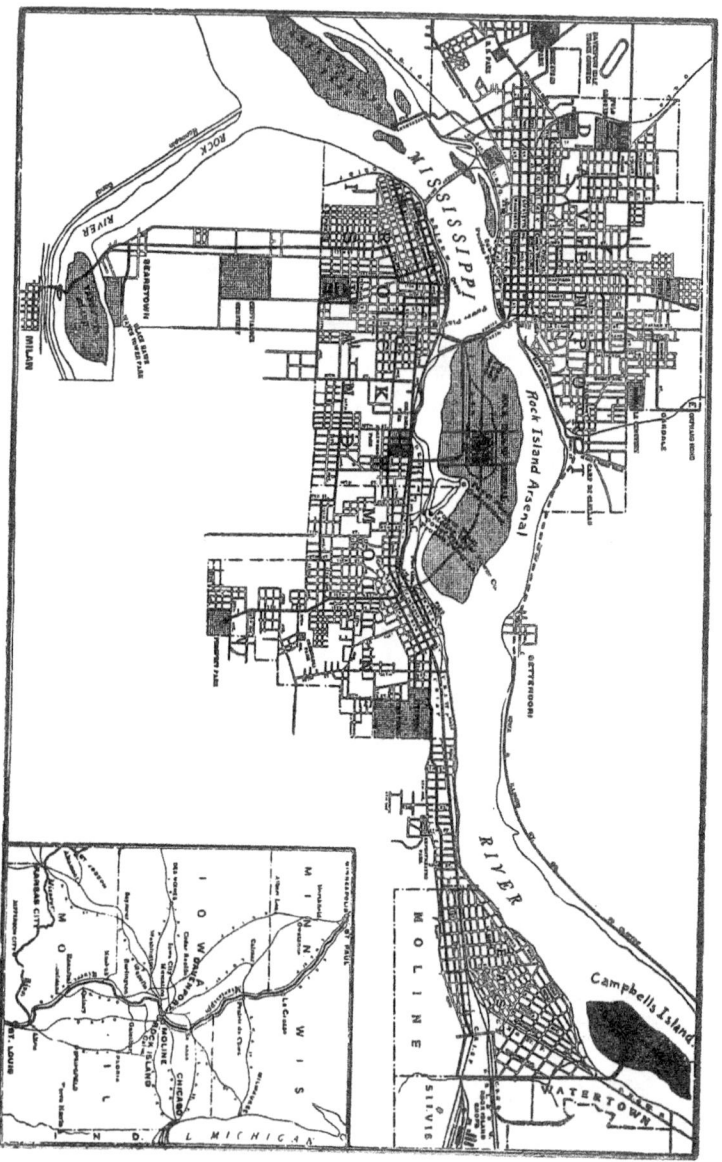

it would get fast in the rapids, in which case they were sure of taking her. They had summoned her on her way down to surrender, but she refused to do so, and now that she had passed the rapids in safety, all hope of taking her had vanished. The British landed a big gun and gave us three soldiers to manage it. They complimented us for our bravery in taking the boat, and told us what they had done at Prairie du Chien. They gave us a keg of rum, and joined with us in our dancing and feasting. We gave them some things we had taken from the boat, particularly books and papers. They started the next morning, promising to return in a few days with a large body of soldiers.

We went to work under the direction of the men left with us, and dug up the ground in two places to put the big gun in, that the men might remain in with it and be safe. We then sent spies down the river to reconnoitre, who sent word by a runner that several boats were coming up filled with men. I marshalled my forces and was soon ready for their arrival. I resolved to fight, as we had not yet had a fair fight with the Americans during the war. The boats arrived in the evening (25), stopping at a small willow island, nearly opposite to us. During the night we removed our big gun farther down, and at daylight next morning commenced firing. We were pleased to see that almost every shot took effect. The British being good gunners, rarely missed. They pushed off as quickly as possible although I had expected they would land and give us battle. I was fully prepared to meet them, but was sadly disappointed by the boats all sailing down the river. A party of braves followed to watch where they landed, but they did not stop until they got below the Des Moines Rapids, where they came ashore and commenced building a fort. I did not want a fort in our country, as we wished to go down to the Two River country in the fall and hunt, it being our choice hunting ground, and we concluded that if this fort was built, it would prevent us from going there. We arrived in the vicinity in the evening, and encamped on a high bluff for the night. We made no fire, for fear of being observed, and our young men kept watch by turns while others slept. I was very tired, and was soon asleep. The Great Spirit, during my slumber, told me to go down the bluff to a creek; that I would there find a hollow tree cut down, and by looking in at the top of it, I would see a large snake with head erect—to observe the direction he was looking, and I would see the enemy close by and unarmed. In the morning I communicated to my braves what the Great Spirit had said to me, took one of them and went down a ravine that led to the creek. I soon came in sight of the place where they were building the fort, which was on a hill at the opposite side of the creek. I saw a great many men. We crawled cautiously on our hands and knees until we got to the bottom land, then through the grass and weeds until we reached the bank of the creek. Here I found a tree that had been cut down; I looked in at the top of it and saw a large snake, with its head raised, looking across the creek. I raised myself cautiously, and discovered nearly opposite me, two war chiefs walking arm in arm, without guns. They turned and walked back toward the place where the men were working at the fort. In a little while they returned, walking directly towards the spot where we lay concealed, but did not come so near as before. If they had they would have been killed, for each of us had a good rifle. We crossed the creek and crawled to a cluster of bushes. I again raised myself a little to see if they were coming; but they went into the fort, and by this they saved their lives.

We recrossed the creek and I returned alone, going up the same ravine I came down. My brave went down the creek, and I on rising to the brow of the hill to the left of the one we came down, could plainly see the men at work. I saw a sentinel walking in the bottom near the mouth of the creek. I watched him attentively, to see if he perceived my companion, who had gone toward him. The sentinel stopped for some time and looked toward where my brave was concealed. He walked first one way and then the other.

I observed my brave creeping towards him, at last he lay still for a while, not even moving the grass, and as the sentinel turned to walk away, my brave fired and he fell. I looked toward the fort, and saw the whites were in great confusion, running wildly in every direction, some down the steep bank toward a boat. My comrade joined me, we returned to the rest of the party and all hurried back to Rock River, where we arrived in safety at our village. I hung up my medicine bag, put away my rifle and spear, feeling as if I should want them no more, as I had no desire to raise other war parties against the whites unless they gave me provocation. Nothing happened worthy of note until spring, except that the fort below the rapids had been abandoned and burned by the Americans.

CHAPTER VII.

GOMO'S STORY—BLACK HAWK TOUCHES THE GOOSE QUILL —HIS OPINION OF AMERICAN DEALINGS—THE INDIANS' GUARDIAN SPIRIT AT FORT ARMSTRONG ON ROCK ISLAND.

Soon after I returned from my wintering ground we received information that peace had been made between the British and Americans, and that we were required to make peace also, and were invited to go down to Portage des Sioux, for that purpose. Some advised that we should go down, others that we should not. Nomite, our principal civil chief, said he would go, as soon as the Foxes came down from the mines.

They came and we all started from Rock River, but we had not gone far before our chief was taken sick and we stopped with him at the village on Henderson River. The Foxes went on and we were to follow as soon as our chief got better, but he rapidly became worse and soon died. His brother now became the principal chief. He refused to go down, saying that if he started, he would be taken sick and die as his brother had done. This seemed to be reasonable, so we concluded that none of us would go at this time. The Foxes returned. They said, "We have smoked the pipe of peace with our enemies, and expect that the Americans will send a war party against you if you do not go down." This I did not believe, as the Americans had always lost by their armies that were sent against us. La Gutrie and other British traders arrived at our village in the fall. La Gutrie told that we must go down and make peace, as this was the wish of our English father. He said he wished us to go down to the Two River country to winter, where game was plenty, as there had been no hunting there for several years.

Having heard the principal war chief had come up with a number of troops, and commenced the erection of a fort near the Rapids des Moines, we consented to go down with the traders to visit the American chief and tell him the reason why we had not been down sooner. When we arrived at the head of the rapids, the traders left their goods, and all of their boats with one exception, in which they accompanied us to see the Americans. We visited the war chief on board his boat, telling him what we had to say, and explaining why we had not been down sooner. He appeared angry and talked to La Gutrie for some time. I inquired of him what the war chief said. He told me that he was threatening to hang him up to the yardarm of his boat. "But," said he, "I am not afraid of what he says. He dare not put his threats into execution. I have done no more than I had a right to do as a British subject."

I then addressed the chief, asking permission for ourselves and some Menomonees, to go down to the Two River country for the purpose of hunting. He said we might go down but must return before the ice came, as he did not intend that we should winter below the fort. "But," he inquired, "what do you want the Menomonees to go with you for?"

I did not know at first what reply to make, but told him that they had a great many pretty squaws with them, and we wished them to go with us on that account. He consented. We all went down the river and remained all winter, as we had no intention of returning before spring when we asked leave to go. We made a good hunt. Having loaded our trader's boats with furs and peltries, they started to Mackinac, and we returned to our village.

There is one circumstance that I did not relate at the proper place. It has no reference to myself or people, but to my friend Gomo, the Pottawattomie chief. He came to Rock River to pay me a visit, and during his stay he related to me the following story:

"The war chief at Peoria is a very good man. He always speaks the truth and treats our people well. He sent for me one day, told me he was nearly out of provisions, and wished me to send my young men hunting to supply his fort. I promised to do so, immediately returned to my camp and told my young men the wishes and wants of the war chief. They readily agreed to go and hunt for our friend and returned with plenty of deer. They carried them to the fort, laid them down at the gate and returned to our camp. A few days afterward I went again to the fort to see if they wanted any more meat. The chief gave me powder and lead and said he wanted me to send my hunters out again. When I returned to camp, I told my young men that the chief wanted more meat. Matatah, one of my principal braves, said he would take a party and go across the Illinois, about one day's travel, where game was plenty, and make a good hunt for our friend the war chief. He took eight hunters with him, and his wife and several other squaws went with them. They had travelled about half the day in the prairie when they discovered a party of white men coming towards them with a drove of cattle. Our hunters apprehended no danger or they would have kept out of the way of the whites, who had not yet perceived them. Matatah changed his course, as he wished to meet and speak to the whites. As soon as the whites saw our party, some of them put off at full speed, and came up to our hunters. Matatah gave up his gun to them, and endeavored to explain to them that he was friendly and was hunting for the war chief. They were not satisfied with this but fired at and wounded him. He got into the branches of a tree that had blown down, to keep the horses from running over him. He was again fired on several times and badly wounded. He, finding that he would be murdered, and, mortally wounded already, sprang at the man nearest him, seized his gun and shot him from his horse. He then fell, covered with blood from his wounds, and immediately expired. The other hunters being in the rear of Matatah attempted to escape, after seeing their leader so basely murdered by the whites. They were pursued and nearly all of the party killed. My youngest brother brought me the news in the night, he having been with the party and being slightly wounded. He said the whites had abandoned their cattle and gone back towards the settlement. The rest of the night was spent in mourning for our friends. At daylight I blacked my face and started for the fort to see the chief. I met him at the gate and told him what had happened. His countenance changed and I could see sorrow depicted in it for the death of my people. He tried to persuade me that I was mistaken, as he could not believe that the whites would act so cruelly. But when I convinced him, he said to me, 'Those cowards who murdered your people shall be punished.' I told him that my people would have revenge, that they would not trouble any of his people at the fort, as we did not blame him or any of his soldiers, but that a party of my braves would go towards the Wabash to avenge the death of their friends and relations. The next day I took a party of hunters, killed several deer, and left them at the fort gate as I passed."

Here Gomo ended his story. I could relate many similar ones that have come within my own knowledge and observation, but I dislike to look back and bring on sorrow afresh. I will resume my narrative.

The great chief at St. Louis having sent word for us to come down and confirm the treaty, we did not hesitate, but started immediately that we might smoke the peace pipe with him. On our arrival we met the great chiefs in council (26). They explained to us the words of our Great

Father at Washington, accusing us of heinous crimes and many misdemeanors, particularly in not coming down when first invited. We knew very well that our Great Father had deceived us and thereby forced us to join the British, and could not believe that he had put this speech into the mouths of those chiefs to deliver to us. I was not a civil chief and consequently made no reply, but our civil chiefs told the commissioners that, "What you say is a lie. Our Great Father sent us no such speech; he knew that the situation in which we had been placed was caused by him." The white chiefs appeared very angry at this reply and said, "We will break off the treaty and make war against you, as you have grossly insulted us."

Our chiefs had no intention of insulting them and told them so, saying, "We merely wish to explain that you have told us a lie, without any desire to make you angry, in the same manner that you whites do when you do not believe what is told you." The council then proceeded and the pipe of peace was smoked.

Here for the first time, I touched the goose quill to the treaty, not knowing, however, by the act, I consented to give away my village. Had that been explained to me I should have opposed it and never would have signed their treaty, as my recent conduct will clearly prove.

What do we know of the manners, the laws, and the customs of the white people? They might buy our bodies for dissection, and we would touch the goose quill to confirm it and not know what we were doing. This was the case with me and my people in touching the goose quill the first time.

We can only judge of what is proper and right by our standard of what is right and wrong, which differs widely from the whites, if I have been correctly informed. The whites may do wrong all their lives, and then if they are sorry for it when about to die, all is well; but with us it is different. We must continue to do good throughout our lives. If we have corn and meat, and know of a family that have none, we divide with them. If we have more blankets than we absolutely need, and others have not enough, we must give to those who are in want. But I will presently explain our customs and the manner in which we live.

We were treated friendly by the whites and started on our return to our village on Rock River. When we arrived we found that the troops had come to build a fort on Rock Island. This, in our opinion, was a contradiction to what we had done—"to prepare for war in time of peace." We did not object, however, to their building their fort on the island, but were very sorry, as this was the best one on the Mississippi, and had long been the resort of our young people during the summer. It was our garden, such as the white people have near their big villages, which supplied us with strawberries, blackberries, gooseberries, plums, apples and nuts of different kinds. Being situated at the foot of the rapids, its waters supplied us with the finest fish. In my early life I spent many happy days on this island. A good spirit had charge of it (27), which lived in a cave in the rocks immediately under the place where the fort now stands. This guardian spirit has often been seen by our people. It was white, with large wings like a swan's, but ten times larger. We were particular not to make much noise in that part of the island which it inhabited, for fear of disturbing it. But the noise at the fort has since driven it away, and no doubt a bad spirit has taken its place.

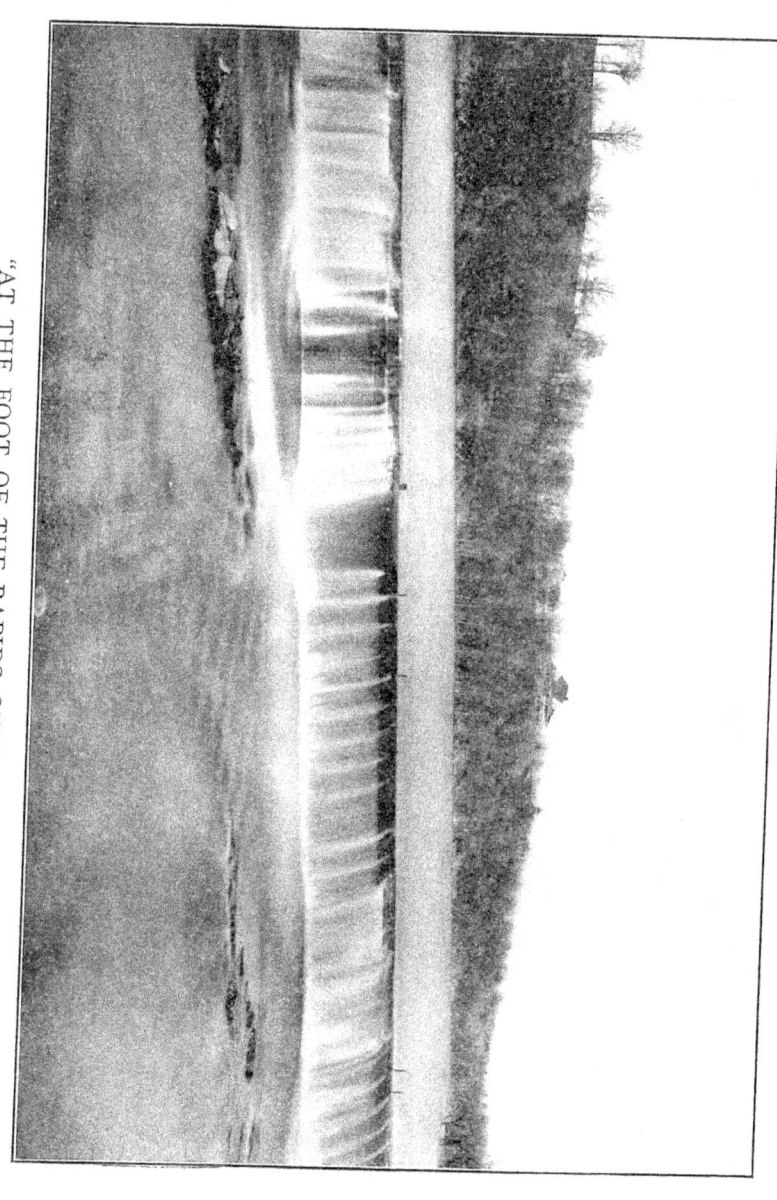

"AT THE FOOT OF THE RAPIDS ON ROCK RIVER."

CHAPTER VIII.

BLACK HAWK'S WATCH TOWER—DESCRIPTION OF THE COUNTRY—INDIAN COURTSHIP AND MARRIAGE CUSTOMS—UNHAPPY REFLECTIONS—INDIAN MODE OF LIFE—DANCES AND AMUSEMENTS—RELIGIOUS BELIEFS—HOW THE CORN CAME—AN INDIAN LOVE TRAGEDY—FORT ARMSTRONG—DEATH OF HIS CHILDREN—RENDITION OF A MURDERER—HIS RELEASE—DEPREDATIONS OF WHITE SETTLERS.

Our village was situated on the north side of Rock River, at the foot of the rapids, on the point of land between Rock River and the Mississippi. In front a prairie extended to the Mississippi, and in the rear a continued bluff gently ascended from the prairie.

On its highest peak our Watch Tower was situated, from which we had a fine view for many miles up and down Rock River, and in every direction. On the side of this bluff we had our cornfields, extending about two miles up parallel with the larger river, where they adjoined those of the Foxes, whose village was on the same stream, opposite the lower end of Rock Island, and three miles distant from ours. We had eight hundred acres in cultivation including what we had on the islands in Rock River. The land around our village which remained unbroken was covered with blue grass which furnished excellent pasture for our horses. Several fine springs poured out of the bluff near by, from which we were well supplied with good water. The rapids of Rock River furnished us with an abundance of excellent fish, and the land being very fertile, never failed to produce good crops of corn, beans, pumpkins, and squashes. We always had plenty; our children never cried from hunger, neither were our people in want.

Here our village had stood for more than a hundred years, during all of which time we were the undisputed possessors of the Mississippi Valley, from the Wisconsin to the Portage des Sioux, near the mouth of the Missouri, being about seven hundred miles in length.

At this time we had very little intercourse with the whites except those who were traders. Our village was healthy, and there was no place in the country possessing such advantages, nor hunting grounds better than those we had in possession. If a prophet had come to our village in those days and told us that the things were to take place which have since come to pass, none of our people would have believed him. What! to be driven from our village and our hunting grounds, and not even to be permitted to visit the graves of our forefathers and relatives and friends?

This hardship is not known to the whites. With us it is a custom to visit the graves of our friends and keep them in repair for many years. The mother will go alone to weep over the grave of her child. The brave, with pleasure, visits the grave of his father, after he has been successful in war, and repaints the post that marks where he lies. There is no place like that where the bones of our forefathers lie to go to when in grief. Here prostrate by the tombs of our fathers will the Great Spirit take pity on us.

But how different our situation now from what it was in those happy days! Then we were as happy as the buffalo on the plains, but now, we are as miserable as the hungry wolf on the prairie. But I am digressing from my story. Bitter reflections crowd upon my mind and must find utterance.

When we returned to our village in the spring, from our wintering grounds, we would finish bartering with our traders, who always followed us to our village. We purposely kept some of our fine furs for this trade, and, as there was great opposition among them who should get these furs, we always got our goods cheap. After this trade was over, the traders would give us a few kegs of rum, which were generally promised in the fall, to encourage us to make a good hunt and not go to war. They would then start with their furs and peltries for their homes, and our old men would take a frolic. At this time our young men never drank. When this was ended, the next thing to be done was to bury our dead; such as had died during the year. This is a great medicine feast. The relations of those who have died, give all the goods they have purchased, as presents to their friends, thereby reducing themselves to poverty, to show the Great Spirit that they are humble, so that he will take pity on them. We would next open the caches (28), take out the corn and other provisions which had been put up in the fall. We would then commence repairing our lodges. As soon as this was accomplished, we repaired the fences around our cornfields and cleaned them off ready for planting. This work was done by the women (29). The men during this time are feasting on dried venison, bear's meat, wild fowl and corn prepared in different ways, while recounting to one another what took place during the winter.

Our women plant the corn, and as soon as they are done we make a feast, at which we dance the crane dance in which they join us, dressed in their most gaudy attire, and decorated with feathers. At this feast the young men select the women they wish to have for wives. Each then informs his mother, who calls on the mother of the girl, when the necessary arrangements are made and the time appointed for him to come. He goes to the lodge when all are asleep, or pretend to be, and with his flint and steel strikes a light and soon finds where his intended sleeps. He then awakens her, holds the light close to his face that she may know him, after which he places the light close to her. If she blows it out the ceremony is ended and he appears in the lodge next morning as one of the family. If she does not blow out the light, but leaves it burning he retires from the lodge. The next day he places himself in full view of it and plays his flute. The young women go out one by one to see who he is playing for. The tune changes to let them know that he is not playing for them. When his intended makes her appearance at the door, he continues his courting tune until she returns to the lodge. He then quits playing and makes another trial at night which usually turns out favorably. During the first year they ascertain whether they can agree with each other and be happy, if not they separate and each looks for another companion. If we were to live together and disagree we would be as foolish as the whites. No indiscretion can banish a woman from her parental lodge; no difference how many children she may bring home she is always welcome—the kettle is over the fire to feed them.

The crane dance often lasts two or three days. When this is over, we feast again and have our national dance. The large square in the village is swept and prepared for the purpose. The chiefs and old warriors take seats on mats, which have been spread on the upper end of the square, next come the drummers and singers, the braves and women form the sides, leaving a large space in the middle. The drums beat and the singing commences. A warrior enters the square, keeping time with the music. He shows the manner he started on a war party, how he approached the enemy, he strikes and shows how he killed him. All join in the applause, and he then leaves the square and another takes his place. Such of our young men as have not been out in war parties and killed an enemy stand back ashamed, not being allowed to enter the square. I remember that I was ashamed to look where our young men stood, before I could take my stand in the ring as a warrior.

What pleasure it is to an old warrior to see his son come forward and relate his exploits. It makes him feel young, induces him to enter the square and "fight his battles o'er again."

This national dance makes our warriors. When I was travelling last summer on a steamboat, on the river going from New York to Albany, I was shown the place where the Americans dance the war dance [West Point], where the old warriors recount to their young men what they have done to stimulate them to go and do likewise. This surprised me, as I did not think the whites understood our way of making braves.

When our national dance is over, our cornfields hoed, every weed dug up and our corn about knee high, all our young men start in a direction toward sundown, to hunt deer and buffalo and to kill Sioux if any are found on our hunting grounds. A part of our old men and women go to the lead mines to make lead, and the remainder of our people start to fish and get meat stuff. Every one leaves the village and remains away about forty days. They then return, the hunting party bringing in dried buffalo and deer meat, and sometimes Sioux scalps, when they are found trespassing on our hunting grounds. At other times they are met by a party of Sioux too strong for them and are driven in. If the Sioux have killed the Sacs last, they expect to be retaliated upon and will fly before them, and so with us. Each party knows that the other has a right to retaliate, which induces those who have killed last to give way before their enemy, as neither wishes to strike, except to avenge the death of relatives. All our wars are instigated by the relations of those killed, or by aggressions on our hunting grounds. The party from the lead mines brings lead, and the others dried fish, and mats for our lodges. Presents are now made by each party, the first giving to the others dried buffalo and deer, and they in return pre-

BLACK HAWK'S AUTOBIOGRAPHY 67

senting them lead, dried fish and mats. This is a happy season of the year, having plenty of provisions, such as beans, squashes and other produce; with our dried meat and fish, we continue to make feasts and visit each other until our corn is ripe. Some lodge in the village makes a feast daily to the Great Spirit. I cannot explain this so that the white people will understand me, as we have no regular standard among us.

Every one makes his feast as he thinks best, to please the Great Spirit, who has the care of all beings created. Others believe in two Spirits, one good and one bad, and make feasts for the Bad Spirit, to keep him quiet. They think that if they can make peace with him, the Good Spirit will not hurt them. For my part I am of the opinion, that so far as we have reason we have a right to use it in determining what is right or wrong, and we should always pursue that path which we believe to be right, believing "whatever is, is right." If the Great and Good Spirit wished us to believe and do as the whites, he could easily change our opinions, so that we could see, and think, and act as they do. We are nothing compared to his power, and we feel and know it. We have men among us, like the whites, who pretend to know the right path, but will not consent to show it without pay. I have no faith in their paths, but believe that every man must make his own path.

When our corn is getting ripe, our young people watch with anxiety for the signal to pull roasting ears, as none dare touch them until the proper time. When the corn is fit for use another great ceremony takes place, with feasting and returning thanks to the Great Spirit for giving us corn.

I will here relate the manner in which corn first came. According to tradition handed down to our people, a beautiful woman was seen to descend from the clouds, and alight upon the earth, by two of our ancestors who had

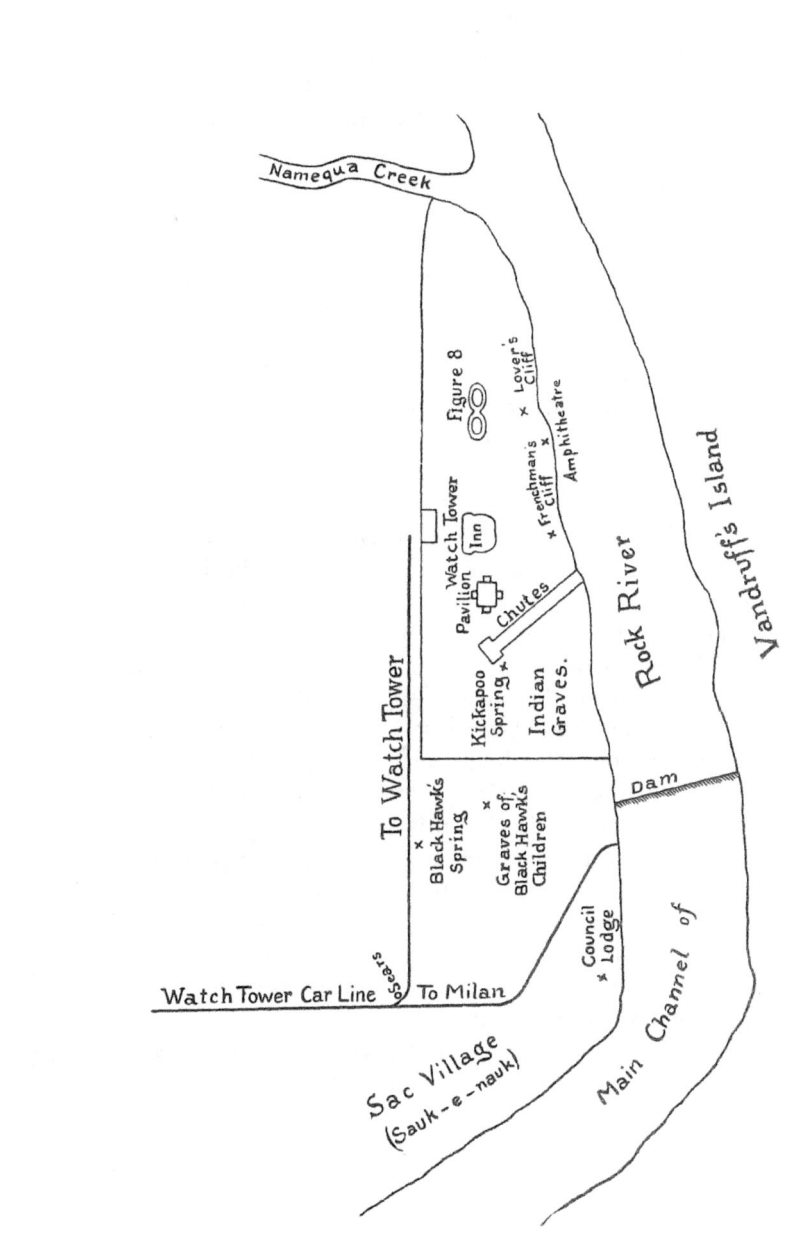

killed a deer, and were sitting by a fire roasting a part of it to eat. They were astonished at seeing her, and concluded that she was hungry and had smelt the meat. They immediately went to her, taking with them a piece of the roasted venison. They presented it to her, she ate it, telling them to return to the spot where she was sitting at the end of one year, and they would find a reward for their kindness and generosity. She then ascended to the clouds and disappeared. The men returned to their village, and explained to the tribe what they had seen, done and heard, but were laughed at by their people. When the period had arrived for them to visit this consecrated ground, where they were to find a reward for their attention to the beautiful woman of the clouds, they went with a large party, and found where her right hand had rested on the ground, corn growing; where the left hand had rested, beans; and immediately where she had been seated, tobacco.

The two first have ever since been cultivated by our people as our principal provisions, and the last is used for smoking. The white people have since found out the latter, and seem to relish it as much as we do, as they use it in different ways, namely: smoking, snuffing and chewing.

We thank the Great Spirit for all the good he has conferred upon us. For myself, I never take a drink of water from a spring without being mindful of His goodness.

We next have our great ball play. From three to five hundred on a side play this game. We play for guns, lead, horses and blankets, or any other kind of property we may have. The successful party takes the stakes, and all return to our lodges with peace and friendship. We next commence horse racing, and continue our sport and feasting until the corn is secured. We then prepare to leave our village for our hunting grounds.

The traders arrive and give us credit for guns, flints, powder, shot and lead, and such articles as we want to clothe our families with and enable us to hunt. We first, however, hold a council with them, to ascertain the price they will give us for our skins, and then they will charge us for the goods. We inform them where we intend hunting, and tell them where to build their houses. At this place we deposit a part of our corn, and leave our old people. The traders have always been kind to them and relieved them when in want, and consequently were always much respected by our people, and never since we were a nation, has one of them been killed by our people.

We then disperse in small parties to make our hunt, and as soon as it is over, we return to our trader's establishment, with our skins, and remain feasting, playing cards and at other pastimes until the close of the winter. Our young men then start on the beaver hunt, others to hunt raccoons and muskrats; the remainder of our people go to the sugar camps to make sugar. All leave our encampment and appoint a place to meet on the Mississippi, so that we may return together to our village in the spring. We always spend our time pleasantly at the sugar camp. It being the season for wild fowl, we lived well and always had plenty, when the hunters came in that we might make a feast for them. After this is over we return to our village, accompanied sometimes by our traders. In this way the time rolled round happily. But these are times that were.

While on the subject of our manners and customs, it might be well to relate an instance that occurred near our village just five years before we left it for the last time.

In 1827, a young Sioux Indian got lost on the prairie, in a snowstorm, and found his way into a camp of the Sacs. According to Indian customs, although he was an enemy, he was safe while accepting their hospitality. He remained there for some time on account of the severity of the storm. Becoming well acquainted, he fell in love with

the daughter of the Sac at whose village he had been entertained, and before leaving for his own country, promised to come to the Sac village for her at a certain time during the approaching summer. In July he made his way to the Rock River village, secreting himself in the woods until he met the object of his love, who came out to the field with her mother to assist her in hoeing corn. Late in the afternoon her mother left her and went to the village. No sooner had she got out of hearing than he gave a loud whistle which assured the maiden that he had returned. She continued hoeing leisurely to the end of the row, when her lover came to meet her, and she promised to come to him as soon as she could go to the lodge and get her blanket, and together they would flee to his country. But unfortunately for the lovers the girl's two brothers had seen the meeting, and after procuring their guns started in pursuit of them. A heavy thunderstorm was coming on at the time. The lovers hastened to and took shelter under a cliff of rocks, at Black Hawk's watch tower. Soon after a loud peal of thunder was heard, the cliff of rocks was shattered in a thousand pieces, and the lovers buried beneath, while in full view of her pursuing brothers.

This, their unexpected tomb, still remains undisturbed.

This tower to which my name had been applied was a favorite resort and was frequently visited by me alone, when I could sit and smoke my pipe, and look with wonder and pleasure at the grand scenes that were presented by the sun's rays, even across the mighty water. On one occasion a Frenchman, who had been making his home in our village, brought his violin with him to the tower, to play and dance for the amusement of a number of our people, who had assembled there, and while dancing with his back to the cliff, accidentally fell over it and was killed by the fall. The Indians say that always at the same time of the year, soft strains of the violin can be heard near that spot.

On returning in the spring from our hunting grounds, I had the pleasure of meeting our old friend, the trader of Peoria, at Rock Island. He came up in a boat from St. Louis, not as a trader, but as our agent. We were well pleased to see him. He told us that he narrowly escaped falling into the hands of Dixon. He remained with us a short time, gave us good advice and then returned to St. Louis.

The Sioux having committed depredations on our people, we sent out war parties that summer, who succeeded in killing fourteen.

I paid several visits to Fort Armstrong, at Rock Island, during the summer, and was always well received by the gentlemanly officers stationed there, who were distinguished for their bravery, and they never trampled upon an enemy's rights. Col. George Davenport resided near the garrison, and being in connection with the American Fur Company, furnished us the greater portion of our goods. We were not as happy then, in our village, as formerly. Our people got more liquor from the small traders than customary. I used all my influence to prevent drunkenness, but without effect. As the settlements progressed toward us we became worse off and more unhappy.

Many of our people, instead of going to the hunting grounds, when game was plenty, would go near the settlements to hunt, and, instead of saving their skins, to pay the trader for goods furnished them in the fall, would sell them to the settlers for whisky, and return in the spring with their families almost naked, and without the means of getting anything for them.

About this time my eldest son was taken sick and died. He had always been a dutiful child and had just grown to manhood. Soon after, my youngest daughter, an interesting and affectionate child, died also. This was a hard stroke, because I loved my children. In my distress I left the noise of the village and built my lodge on a mound in the cornfield (30), and enclosed it with a fence, around which I planted corn and beans. Here I was with my family alone. I gave everything I had away, and reduced myself to poverty. The only covering I retained was a piece of buffalo robe. I blacked my face and resolved on fasting for twenty-four moons, for the loss of my two children—drinking only of water during the day, and eating sparingly of boiled corn at sunset. I fulfilled my promise, hoping that the Great Spirit would take pity on me.

My nation had now some difficulty with the Iowas. Our young men had repeatedly killed some of them, and the breaches had always been made up by giving presents to the relations of those killed. But the last council we had with them, we promised that in case any more of their people were killed by ours, instead of presents, we would give up the person or persons, who had done the injury. We made this determination known to our people, but notwithstanding this, one of our young men killed an Iowa the following winter.

A party of our people were about starting for the Iowa village to give the young man up, and I agreed to accompany them. When we were ready to start, I called at the lodge for the young man to go with us. He was sick, but willing to go, but his brother, however, prevented him and insisted on going to die in his place, as he was unable to travel. We started, and on the seventh day arrived in sight of the Iowa village, and within a short distance of it we halted and dismounted. We all bid farewell to our young brave, who entered the village singing his death song, and sat down on the square in the middle of the village. One of the Iowa chiefs came out to us. We told him that we had fulfilled our promise, that we had brought the brother of the young man who had killed one of his people—that he had volunteered to come in his place, in consequence of his brother being unable to travel from sickness. We had no further conversation, but mounted our horses and rode off. As we started I cast my eye toward the village, and observed the Iowas coming out of their lodges with spears and war clubs. We took the backward trail and travelled until dark—then encamped and made a fire. We had not been there long before we heard the sound of horses coming toward us. We seized our arms; but instead of an enemy it was our young brave with two horses. He told me that after we had left him, they menaced him with death for some time—then gave him something to eat—smoked the pipe with him and made him a present of the two horses and some goods, and started him after us. When we arrived at our village our people were much pleased, and for their noble and generous conduct on this occasion, not one of the Iowa people has been killed since by our nation.

That fall I visited Malden with several of my band, and was well treated by the agent of our British Father, who gave us a variety of presents. He also gave me a medal, and told me there never would be war between England and America again; but for my fidelity to the British, during the war that had terminated some time before, requested me to come with my band and get presents every year, as Colonel Dixon had promised me.

I returned and hunted that winter on the Two Rivers. The whites were now settling the country fast. I was out one day hunting in a bottom, and met three white men. They accused me of killing their hogs. I denied it, but they would not listen to me. One of them took my gun out of my hand and fired it off—then took out the flint, gave it back to me and commenced beating me with sticks, ordering me at the same time to be off. I was so much bruised that I could not sleep for several nights.

Some time after this occurrence, one of my camp cut

a bee tree and carried the honey to his lodge. A party of white men soon followed him, and told him the bee tree was theirs, and that he had no right to cut it. He pointed to the honey and told them to take it. They were not satisfied with this, but took all the packs of skins that he had collected during the winter, to pay his trader and clothe his family with in the spring, and carried them off.

How could we like a people who treated us so unjustly? We determined to break up our camp, for fear they would do worse, and when we joined our people in the spring a great many of them complained of similar treatment.

CHAPTER IX.

AMERICANS PREPARE TO ENFORCE THE TREATY OF 1804—
COLONEL DAVENPORT ADVISES THE SACS—KEOKUK
LEAVES SAUKENAUK—BLACK HAWK HOLDS THE WATCH
TOWER—JUDGE PENCE IN BLACK HAWK'S WIGWAM—
INDIAN IDEAS OF LAND TITLES—BLACK HAWK'S TEMPERANCE CRUSADE—MORE WHITE DEPREDATIONS—LE-
CLAIRE MARKED FOR SLAUGHTER—COLONEL DAVENPORT
BUYS THE WATCH TOWER.

This summer our agent came to live at Rock Island. He treated us well and gave us good advice. I visited him and the trader very often during the summer, and for the first time heard talk of our having to leave our village. The trader, Col. George Davenport, who spoke our language, explained to me the terms of the treaty that had been made, and said we would be obliged to leave the Illinois side of the Mississippi, and advised us to select a good place for our village and remove to it in the spring. He pointed out the difficulties we would have to encounter if we remained at our village on Rock River. He had great influence with the principal Fox chief, his adopted brother, Keokuk. He persuaded him to leave his village, go to the west side of the Mississippi and build another, which he did the spring following. Nothing was talked of but leaving our village. Keokuk had been persuaded to consent to go, and was using his influence, backed by the war chief at Fort Armstrong and our agent and trader at Rock Island, to induce others to go with him. He sent the crier through our village, to inform our people that it was the wish of our Great Father that we should remove to the west side of the Mississippi, and recommended the Iowa River as a good place for the new village. He wished his party to make such arrangements, before they started on their winter's hunt, as to preclude the necessity of their returning to the village in the spring.

The party opposed to removing called on me for my opinion. I gave it freely, and after questioning Quashqua-me about the sale of our lands, he assured me that he "never had consented to the sale of our village." I now promised this party to be the leader, and raised the standard of opposition to Keokuk, with a full determination not to leave our village. I had an interview with Keokuk, to see if this difficulty could not be settled with our Great Father, and told him to propose to give any other land that our Great Father might choose, even our lead mines, to be peaceably permitted to keep the small point of land on which our village was situated. I was of the opinion that the white people had plenty of land and would never take our village from us. Keokuk promised to make an exchange if possible, and applied to our agent, and the great chief at St. Louis, who had charge of all the agents, for permission to go to Washington for that purpose.

This satisfied us for a time. We started to our hunting grounds with good hopes that something would be done for us. During the winter I received information that three families of whites had come to our village and destroyed some of our lodges, were making fences and dividing our cornfields for their own use. They were quarreling among themselves about their lines of division. I started immediately for Rock River, a distance of ten days' travel, and on my arrival found the report true. I went to my lodge and found a family occupying it. I wished to talk to them, but they could not understand me (31). I then went to Rock Island; the agent being absent, I told the interpreter what I wanted to say to these people, viz.: "Not to settle on our lands, nor trouble our fences, that there was plenty of land in the country for them to settle upon, and that

BLACK HAWK'S AUTOBIOGRAPHY

they must leave our village, as we were coming back to it in the spring." The interpreter wrote me a paper; I went back to the village and showed it to the intruders, but could not understand their reply. I presumed, however, that they would remove as I expected them to. I returned to Rock Island, passed the night there, and had a long conversation with the trader. He advised me to give up and make my village with Keokuk on the Iowa River. I told him that I would not. The next morning I crossed the Mississippi on very bad ice, but the Great Spirit had made it strong, that I might pass over safe. I traveled three days farther to see the Winnebago sub-agent and converse with him about our difficulties. He gave no better news than the trader had done. I then started by way of Rock River, to see the prophet, believing that he was a man of great knowledge. When we met, I explained to him everything as it was. He at once agreed that I was right, and advised me never to give up our village, for the whites to plow up the bones of our people. He said that if we remained at our village the whites would not trouble us, and advised me to get Keokuk, and the party that consented to go with him to the Iowa in the spring, to return and remain at our village.

I returned to my hunting ground, after an absence of one moon, and related what I had done. In a short time we came up to our village, and found that the whites had not left it, but that others had come, and that the greater part of our cornfields had been enclosed. When we landed the whites appeared displeased because we came back. We repaired the lodges that had been left standing and built others. Keokuk came to the village; but his object was to persuade others to follow him to the Iowa. He had accomplished nothing towards making arrangements for us to remain, or to exchange other lands for our village. There was no more friendship existing between us. I looked upon him as a coward and no brave, to abandon his village to be occupied by strangers. What right had these people to our village, and our fields, which the Great Spirit had given us to live upon?

During this summer I happened at Rock Island, when a great chief arrived, whom I had known as the great chief of Illinois (Governor Cole) in company with another chief, who I have been told is a great writer (Judge James Hall). I called upon them and begged to explain the grievances to them, under which my people and I were laboring, hoping that they could do something for us. The great chief, however, did not seem disposed to council with me. He said he was no longer the chief of Illinois; that his children had selected another father in his stead, and that he now only ranked as they did. I was surprised at this talk, as I had always heard that he was a good brave and great chief. But the white people appear to never be satisfied. When they get a good father they hold councils at the suggestion of some bad, ambitious man, who wants the place himself, and conclude among themselves that this man, or some other equally ambitious, would make a better father than they have, and nine times out of ten they don't get as good a one again.

I insisted on explaining to these chiefs the true situation of my people. They gave their assent. I arose and made a speech, in which I explained to them the treaty made by Quasnquame and three of our braves, according to the manner the trader and others had explained it to me. I then told them that Quashquame and his party positively denied having ever sold my village, and that as I had never known them to lie, I was determined to keep it in possession.

I told them that the white people had already entered our village, burned our lodges, destroyed our fences, ploughed up our corn and beat our people. They had brought whisky into our country, made our people drunk, and taken from them their horses, guns and traps, and that I had borne all this injury, without suffering any of my braves to raise a hand against the whites.

My object in holding this council was to get the opinion of these two chiefs as to the best course for me to pursue. I had appealed in vain, time after time to our agent, who regularly represented our situation to the chief at St. Louis, whose duty it was to call upon the Great Father to have justice done to us, but instead of this we are told that the white people wanted our country and we must leave it for them!

I did not think it possible that our Great Father wished us to leave our village where we had lived so long, and where the bones of so many of our people had been laid. The great chief said that as he no longer had any authority he could do nothing for us, and felt sorry that it was not in his power to aid us, nor did he know how to advise us. Neither of them could do anything for us, but both evidently were very sorry. It would give me great pleasure at all times to take these two chiefs by the hand.

That fall I paid a visit to the agent before we started to our hunting grounds, to hear if he had any good news for me. He had news. He said that the land on which our village now stood was ordered to be sold to individuals, and that when sold our right to remain by treaty would be at an end, and that if we returned next spring we would be forced to remove.

We learned during the winter that part of the land where our village stood had been sold to individuals, and that the trader at Rock Island, Colonel Davenport, had bought the greater part that had been sold. The reason was now plain to me why he urged us to remove. His object, we thought, was to get our lands. We held several councils that winter to determine what we should do. We resolved in one of them to return to our village as usual in the spring. We concluded that if we were removed by force that the trader, agent and others must be the cause, and that if they were found guilty of having driven us from our village they should be killed. The trader stood foremost on this list. He had purchased the land on which my lodge stood, and that of our graveyard also. We therefore proposed to kill him and the agent, the interpreter, the great chief at St. Louis, the war chief at Fort Armstrong, Rock Island, and Keokuk, these being the principal persons to blame for endeavoring to remove us.

Our women received bad accounts from the women who had been raising corn at the new village, of the difficulty of breaking the new prairie with hoes, and the small quantity of corn raised. We were nearly in the same condition with regard to the latter, it being the first time I ever knew our people to be in want of provisions.

I prevailed upon some of Keokuk's band to return this spring to Rock River village, but Keokuk himself would not come. I hoped that he would get permission to go to Washington to settle our affairs with our Great Father. I visited the agent at Rock Island. He was displeased because we had returned to our village, and told me that we must remove to the west of the Mississippi. I told him plainly that we would not. I visited the interpreter at his house, who advised me to do as the agent had directed me. I then went to see the trader and upbraided him for buying our lands. He said that if he had not purchased them some person else would, and that if our Great Father would make an exchange with us, he would willingly give up the land he had purchased to the government. This I thought was fair, and began to think that he had not acted as badly as I had suspected. We again repaired our lodges and built others, as most of our village had been burnt and destroyed. Our women selected small patches to plant corn, where the whites had not taken them in their fences, and worked hard to raise something for our children to subsist upon.

I was told that according to the treaty we had no right to remain on the lands sold, and that the government would force us to leave them. There was but a small portion, however, that had been sold, the balance remaining in the hands of the government. We claimed the right, if we had no other, to "live and hunt upon it as long as it remained the property of the government," by a stipulation in the treaty that required us to evacuate it after it had been sold. This was the land that we wished to inhabit and thought we had a right to occupy.

I heard that there was a great chief on the Wabash, and sent a party to get his advice. They informed him that we had not sold our village. He assured them then, that if we had not sold the land on which our village stood, our Great Father would not take it from us.

I started early to Malden to see the chief of my British Father, and told him my story. He gave the same reply that the chief on the Wabash had given, and in justice to him I must say he never gave me any bad advice, but advised me to apply to our American Father, who, he said, would do us justice. I next called on the great chief at Detroit and made the same statement to him that I had made to the chief of our British Father. He gave me the same reply. He said if we had not sold our lands, and would remain peaceably on them, that we would not be disturbed. This assured me that I was right, and determined me to hold out as I had promised my people. I returned from Malden late in the fall. My people were gone to their hunting ground, whither I followed. Here I learned that they had been badly treated all summer by the whites, and that a treaty had been held at Prairie du Chien. Keokuk and some of our people attended it, and found that our Great Father had exchanged a small strip of the land that

NAM-E-QUA CREEK.

had been ceded by Quashquame and his party, with the Pottawattomies for a portion of their land near Chicago. That the object of this treaty was to get it back again, and that the United States had agreed to give them sixteen thousand dollars a year forever for this small strip of land, it being less than a twentieth part of that taken from our nation for one thousand dollars a year. This bears evidence of something I cannot explain. This land they say belonged to the United States. What reason then, could have induced them to exchange it with the Pottawattomies if it was so valuable? Why not keep it? Or if they found they had made a bad bargain with the Pottawattomies, why not take back their land at a fair proportion of what they gave our nation for it? If this small portion of the land that they took from us for one thousand dollars a year, be worth sixteen thousand dollars a year forever to the Pottawattomies, then the whole tract of country taken from us ought to be worth, to our nation, twenty times as much as this small faction.

Here I was again puzzled to find out how the white people reasoned and begun to doubt whether they had any standard of right and wrong.

CHAPTER X.

A DIVIDED PEOPLE—INDIAN POLITICS—THE WHITES PLOUGH UP THE INDIAN CORNFIELDS—A TERRIFYING DANCE—A FRUITLESS COUNCIL—GENERAL GAINES MOVES UP TO ROCK RIVER—ARRIVAL OF THE MILITIA—DESTRUCTION OF SAUKENAUK—THE LAW OF RETALIATION.

Communication was kept up between myself and the prophet. Runners were sent to the Arkansas, Red River and Texas, not on the subject of our lands, but on a secret mission which I am not at present permitted to explain.

It was related to me that the chiefs and head men of the Foxes had been invited to Prairie du Chien, to hold a council for the purpose of settling the difficulties existing between them and the Sioux.

The chiefs and head men, amounting to nine, started for the place designated, taking with them one woman, and were met by the Menomonees and Sioux, near the Wisconsin and killed all except one man. Having understood that the whole matter was published shortly after it occurred, and is known to the white people, I will say no more about it.

I would here remark that our pastimes and sports had been laid aside for two years. We were a divided people, forming two parties, Keokuk being at the head of one, willing to barter our rights merely for the good opinion of the whites, and cowardly enough to desert our village to them. I was at the head of the other division and was determined to hold on to my village, although I had been ordered to leave it. But I considered as myself and band had no agency in selling our country, and that, as provision had been made in the treaty, for us all to remain on it as long as it belonged to the United States, that we could not be forced away. I refused, therefore, to quit my village. It was here that I was born, and here lie the bones of many friends and relations. For this spot I felt a sacred rever-

83

ence and never could consent to leave it without being forced therefrom.

When I called to mind the scenes of my youth and those of later days, when I reflected that the theater on which these were acted had been so long the home of my fathers, who now slept on the hills around it, I could not bring my mind to consent to leave this country to the whites for any earthly consideration.

The winter passed off in gloom. We made a bad hunt for want of guns, traps and other necessaries which the whites had taken from our people for whisky. The prospect before us was a bad one. I fasted and called upon the Great Spirit to direct my steps to the right path. I was in great sorrow because all the whites with whom I was acquainted and had been on terms of intimacy, advised me contrary to my wishes; I began to doubt whether I had a friend among them.

My reason teaches me that land cannot be sold. The Great Spirit gave it to his children to live upon and cultivate as far as necessary for their subsistence, and so long as they occupy and cultivate it they have the right to the soil, but if they voluntarily leave it then any other people have a right to settle on it. Nothing can be sold but such things as can be carried away.

In consequence of the improvements of the intruders on our fields, we found considerable difficulty to get ground to plant a little corn. Some of the whites permitted us to plant small patches in the fields they had fenced, keeping all the best ground for themselves. Our women had great difficulty in climbing their fences, being unaccustomed to the kind, and were ill-treated if they left a rail down.

One of my old friends thought he was safe. His cornfield was on a small island in Rock River. He planted his corn, it came up well, but the white man saw it; he wanted it, and took his teams over, ploughed up the crop and replanted it for himself. The old man shed tears, not for himself, but on account of the distress his family would be in if they raised no corn. The white people brought whisky to our village, made our people drunk, and cheated them out of their horses, guns and traps. This fraudulent system was carried to such an extent that I apprehended serious difficulties might occur, unless a stop was put to it. Consequently I visited all the whites and begged them not to sell my people whisky. One of them continued the practice openly; I took a party of my young men, went to his house, took out his barrel, broke in the head and poured out the whisky. I did this for fear some of the whites might get killed by my people when they were drunk.

Our people were treated very badly by the whites on many occasions. At one time a white man beat one of our women cruelly for pulling a few suckers of corn out of his field to suck when she was hungry. At another time one of our young men was beat with clubs by two white men for opening a fence which crossed our road to take his horse through. His shoulder blade was broken and his body badly bruised, from the effects of which he soon after died.

Bad and cruel as our people were treated by the whites, not one of them was hurt or molested by our band. I hope this will prove that we are a peaceable people—having permitted ten men to take possession of our cornfields, prevent us from planting corn, burn our lodges, ill-treat our women, and beat to death our men without offering resistance to their barbarous cruelties. This is a lesson worthy for the white man to learn: To use forbearance when injured.

We acquainted our agent daily with our situation, and through him the great chief at St. Louis, and hoped that something would be done for us. The whites were complaining at the same time that we were intruding upon their rights. They made it appear that they were the injured party, and we the intruders. They called loudly to the great war chief to protect their property.

How smooth must be the language of the whites, when they can make right look like wrong, and wrong like right.

Keokuk, who has a smooth tongue, and is a great speaker, was busy in persuading my band that I was wrong, and thereby making many of them dissatisfied with me. I had one consolation, for all the women were on my side on account of their cornfields.

On my arrival again at my village with my band increased, I found it worse than before. I visited Rock Island, and the agent again ordered me to quit my village. He said that if we did not, troops would be sent to drive us off. He reasoned with me and told me it would be better for us to be with the rest of our people, so that we might avoid difficulty and live in peace. The interpreter joined him and gave me so many good reasons that I almost wished I had not undertaken the difficult task I had pledged myself to my brave band to perform. In this mood I called upon the trader, who is fond of talking, and had long been my friend, but now amongst those who advised me to give up my village. He received me very friendly and went on to defend Keokuk in what he had done, endeavoring to show me that I was bringing distress on our women and children. He inquired if some terms could not be made that would be honorable to me and satisfactory to my braves, for us to remove to the west side of the Mississippi. I replied that if our Great Father could do us justice, and make the proposition, I could then give up honorably. He asked me "if the great chief at St. Louis would give us six thousand dollars to purchase provisions and other articles, if I would give up peaceably and remove to the west side of the Mississippi." After thinking some time I agreed that I could honorably give up, being paid for it, according to our customs, but told him that I could not make the proposal myself, even if I wished, because it would be dishonorable in me to do so. He said that he would do it by sending word to the great chief at St. Louis that he could remove us peaceably for the amount stated, to the west side of the Mississippi. A steamboat arrived at the island during my stay. After its departure the trader told me that he had requested a war chief, who was stationed at Galena, and was on board the steamboat, to make the offer to the great chief at St. Louis, and that he would soon be back and bring his answer. I did not let my people know what had taken place for fear they would be displeased. I did not much like what had been done myself, and tried to banish it from my mind.

After a few days had passed the war chief returned and brought an answer that "the great chief at St. Louis would give us nothing, and that if we did not remove immediately we would be driven off."

I was not much displeased with the answer they brought me, because I would rather have laid my bones with those of my forefathers than remove for any consideration. Yet if a friendly offer had been made, as I expected, I would, for the sake of our women and children, have removed peaceably.

I now resolved to remain in my village, and make no resistance if the military came, but submit to my fate. I impressed the importance of this course on all my band, and directed them in case the military came not to raise an arm against them.

About this time our agent was put out of office, for what reason I could never ascertain. I then thought it was for wanting to make us leave our village and if so it was right, because I was tired of hearing him talk about it. The interpreter, who had been equally bad in trying to persuade us to leave our village was retained in office, and the young man who took the place of our agent told the same old story over about removing us. I was then satisfied that this could not have been the cause.

Our women had planted a few patches of corn which was growing finely, and promised a subsistence for our children, but the white people again commenced ploughing it up. I now determined to put a stop to it by clearing our country of the intruders. I went to their principal men and told them that they should and must leave our country, giving them until the middle of the next day to remove. The worst left within the time appointed, but the one who remained (32) represented that his family, which was large, would be in a starving condition if he went and left his crop. He promised to behave well if I would consent to let him remain until fall in order to secure his crop. He spoke reasonably and I consented.

We now resumed some of our games and pastimes, having been assured by the prophet that we would not be removed. But in a little while it was ascertained that the great war chief, General Gaines, was on his way to Rock River with a great number of soldiers. I again called upon the prophet, who requested a little time to see into the matter. Early next morning he came to me and said he had been dreaming; that he saw nothing bad in this great war chief, General Gaines, who was now near Rock River; that his object was merely to frighten us from our village, that the white people might get our land for nothing. He assured us that this great war chief dare not, and would not, hurt any of us. That the Americans were at peace with the British, and when they made peace, the British required, and the Americans agreed to it, that they should never interrupt any nation of Indians that was at peace, and that all we had to do to retain our village was to refuse any and every offer that might be made by this war chief.

The war chief arrived and convened a council at the agency. Keokuk and Wapello were sent for, and with a number of their band were present,

The council house was opened and all were admitted, and myself and band were sent for to attend. When we arrived at the door singing a war song, and armed with lances, spears, war clubs, bows and arrows, as if going to battle, I halted and refused to enter, as I could see no necessity or propriety in having the room crowded with those who were already there. If the council was convened for us, why then have others in our room. The war chief having sent all out except Keokuk, Wapello and a few of their chiefs and braves, we entered the council in this warlike appearance, being desirous of showing the war chief that we were not afraid. He then rose and made a speech. He said:

"The president is very sorry to be put to the trouble and expense of sending so large a body of soldiers here to remove you from the lands you have long since ceded to the United States. Your Great Father has already warned you repeatedly, through your agent, to leave the country, and he is very sorry to find that you have disobeyed his orders. Your Great Father wishes you well, and asks nothing from you but what is reasonable and right. I hope you will consult your own interests and leave the country you are occupying, and go to the other side of the Mississippi."

I replied:

"We have never sold our country. We never received any annuities from our American Father, and we are determined to hold on to our village."

The war chief, apparently angry, rose and said:

"Who is Black Hawk? Who is Black Hawk?"

"I am a Sac! My forefather was a Sac! And all the nations call me a SAC!!"

The war chief said:

"I came here neither to beg nor hire you to leave your village. My business is to remove you, peaceably if I can, forcibly if I must! I will now give you two days in which to remove, and if you do not cross the Mississippi by that time, I will adopt measures to force you away."

I told him that I never would consent to leave my village and was determined not to leave it.

The council broke up and the war chief retired to his fort. I consulted the prophet again. He said he had been dreaming, and that the Great Spirit had directed that a woman, the daughter of Mattatas, the old chief of the village, should take a stick in her hand and go before the war chief, and tell him that she is the daughter of Mattatas, and that he had always been the white man's friend. That he had fought their battles, been wounded in their service and had always spoken well of them, and she had never heard him say that he had sold their village. The whites are numerous, and can take it from us if they choose, but she hoped they would not be so unfriendly. If they were, she had one favor to ask; she wished her people to be allowed to remain long enough to gather their provisions now growing in their fields; that she was a woman and had worked hard to raise something to support her children. And now, if we are driven from our village without being allowed to save our corn, many of our little children must perish with hunger.

Accordingly, Mattatas' daughter was sent to the fort, accompanied by several of our young men, and was admitted. She went before the war chief and told the story of the prophet. The war chief said the president did not send him here to make treaties with the women, nor to hold council with them. That our young men must leave the fort, but she might remain if she wished.

All our plans were defeated. We must cross the river, or return to our village and await the coming of the war chief with his soldiers. We determined on the latter, but finding that our agent. interpreter, trader and Keokuk, were determined on breaking my ranks, and had induced several of my warriors to cross the Mississippi, I sent a deputation to the agent, at the request of my band, pledging myself to leave the country in the fall, provided permission was given us to remain and secure our crop of corn then growing, as we would be in a starving situation if we were driven off without the means of subsistence.

I directed my village crier to proclaim that my orders were, in the event of the war chief coming to our village to remove us, that not a gun should be fired or any resistance offered. That if he determined to fight, for them to remain quietly in their lodges and let him kill them if he chose.

I felt confident that this great war chief would not hurt our people, and my object was not war. Had it been we would have attacked and killed the war chief and his braves when in council with us, as they were then completely in our power. But his manly conduct and soldierly deportment, his mild yet energetic manner, which proved his bravery, forbade it.

Some of our young men who had been out as spies came in and reported that they had discovered a large body of mounted men coming toward our village, who looked like a war party. They arrived and took a position below Rock River for their place of encampment. The great war chief, General Gaines, entered Rock River in a steamboat, with his soldiers and one big gun. They passed and returned close by our village, but excited no alarm among my braves. No attention was paid to the boat; even our little children, who were playing on the bank of the river, as usual, continued their amusement. The water being shallow, the boat got aground, which gave the whites some trouble. If they had asked for assistance there was not a brave in my band who would not willingly have aided them. Their people were permitted to pass and repass through our village, and were treated with friendship by our people.

The war chief appointed the next day to remove us. I would have remained and been taken prisoner by the regulars, but was afraid of the multitude of pale faced militia (33), who were under horseback, as they were under no restraint of their chiefs.

We crossed the river during the night, and encamped some distance below Rock Island. The great war chief convened another council for the purpose of making a treaty with us. In this treaty he agreed to give us corn in place of that we had left growing in our fields. I touched the goose quill to this treaty, and was determined to live in peace.

The corn that had been given us was soon found to be inadequate to our wants, when loud lamentations were heard in the camp by the women and children, for their roasting ears, beans and squashes. To satisfy them a small party of braves went over in the night to take corn from their own fields. They were discovered by the whites and fired upon. Complaints were again made of the depredations committed by some of my people, on their own cornfields.

I understood from our agent that there had been a provision made in one of our treaties for assistance in agriculture, and that we could have our fields plowed if we required it. I therefore called upon him, and requested him to have a small log house built for me, and a field plowed that fall, as I wished to live retired. He promised to have it done. I then went to the trader, Colonel Davenport, and asked him for permission to be buried in the graveyard at our village, among my old friends and warriors, which he gave cheerfully. I then returned to my people satisfied.

A short time after this a party of Foxes went up to Prairie du Chien to avenge the murder of their chiefs and relations, which had been committed the summer previous by the Menomonees and Sioux. When they arrived in the vicinity of the encampment of the Menomonees, they met with a Winnebago, and inquired for the Menomonees' camp. They requested him to go on before them and see if there were any Winnebagoes in it, and if so, to tell them that they had better return to their own camp. He went and gave the information not only to the Winnebagoes, but to the Menomonees, that they might be prepared. The party soon followed, killed twenty-eight Menomonees, and made their escape.

This retaliation, which with us is considered lawful and right, created considerable excitement among the whites. A demand was made for the Foxes to be surrendered to, and tried by, the white people. The principal men came to me during the fall and asked my advice. I conceived that they had done right, and that our Great Father acted very unjustly in demanding them, when he had suffered all their chiefs to be decoyed away and murdered by the Menomonees, without ever having made a similar demand of them. If he had no right in the first instance he had none now, and for my part I conceived the right very questionable, if not an act of usurpation in any case, where a difference exists between two nations, for him to interfere. The Foxes joined my band with the intention to go out with them on the fall hunt.

CHAPTER XI.

NEAPOPE (NAWPOPE) GOES TO MALDEN—RETURNS BADLY ADVISED—THE UNYIELDING JACKSON—BLACK HAWK RETURNS TO ROCK RIVER—THE PROPHET GIVES MORE BAD ADVICE—ATKINSON ORDERS BLACK HAWK TO RETURN—COLD RECEPTION FROM THE WINNEBAGOES—SENDS FLAG OF TRUCE TO MAJOR STILLMAN—INDIAN FLAG BEARERS KILLED—STILLMAN'S DEFEAT.

About this time, Neapope, who started to Malden when it was ascertained that the great war chief, General Gaines, was coming to remove us, returned. He said he had seen the chief of our British Father, and asked him if the American could force us to leave our village. He said: "If you had not sold your land the Americans could not take your village from you. That the right being vested in you, only could be transferred by the voice and will of the whole nation, and that as you had never given your consent to the sale of your country, it yet remains your exclusive property, from which the American government never could force you away; and that in the event of war, you should have nothing to fear, as we would stand by and assist you."

He said that he had called at the prophet's lodge on his way down, and there had learned for the first time that we had left our village. He informed me privately that the prophet was anxious to see me, as he had much good news to tell me, and that I would hear good news in the spring from our British Father. "The prophet requested me to give you all the particulars, but I would much rather you would see him yourself and learn all from him. But I will tell you that he has received expresses from our British Father, who says that he is going to send us guns, ammunition (34), provisions and clothing early in the spring.

The vessels that bring them will come by way of Milwaukee. The prophet has likewise received wampum and tobacco from the different nations on the lakes, Ottawas, Chippewas and Pottawattomies, and as to the Winnebagoes he has them all at his command. We are going to be happy once more."

I told him I was pleased that our British Father intended to see us righted. That we had been driven from our lands without receiving anything for them, and I now began to hope from his talk, that my people would once more be happy. If I could accomplish this I would be satisfied. I am now growing old and could spend the remnant of my time anywhere. But I wish first to see my people happy. I can leave them cheerfully. This has always been my constant aim, and I now begin to hope that our sky will soon be clear.

Neapope said:

"The prophet told me that all the tribes mentioned would fight for us if necessary, and the British Father will support us. If we should be whipped, which is hardly possible, we will still be safe, the prophet having received a friendly talk from the chief Wassacummico, at Selkirk's settlement, telling him that if we were not happy in our own country to let him know and he would make us happy. He had received information from our British Father that we had been badly treated by the Americans. We must go and see the prophet. I will go first; you had better remain and get as many of your people to join you as you can. You know everything that we have done. We leave the matter with you to arrange among your people as you please. I will return to the prophet's village tomorrow. You can in the meantime make up your mind as to the course you will take and send word to the prophet by me, as he is anxious to assist us, and wishes to know whether you will join us, and assist to make your people happy."

During the night I thought over everything that Neapope had told me, and was pleased to think that by a little exertion on my part, I could accomplish the object of all my wishes. I determined to follow the advice of the prophet, and sent word by Neapope that I would get all my braves together, explain everything that I had heard to them, and recruit as many as I could from the different villages.

Accordingly I sent word to Keokuk's band and the Fox tribe, explaining to them all the good news I had heard. They would not hear. Keokuk said that I had been imposed upon by liars and had much better remain where I was, and keep quiet. When he found that I was determined to make an attempt to recover my village, fearing that some difficulty would arise, he made application to the agent and great chief at St. Louis, asking permission for the chiefs of our nation to go to Washington to see our Great Father, that we might have our difficulties settled amicably. Keokuk also requested the trader, Colonel Davenport, who was going to Washington, to call on our Great Father and explain everything to him, and ask permission for us to come on and see him.

Having heard nothing favorable from the great chief at St. Louis, I concluded that I had better keep my band together and recruit as many as possible, so that I would be prepared to make the attempt to rescue my village in the spring, providing our Great Father did not send word for us to go to Washington. The trader returned (35). He said he had called on our Great Father and made a full statement to him in relation to our difficulties, and had asked leave for us to go to Washington, but had received no answer.

I had determined to listen to the advice of my friends, and if permitted to go to see our Great Father, to abide by his counsel, whatever it might be. Every overture was

BLACK HAWK'S AUTOBIOGRAPHY   97

made by Keokuk to prevent difficulty, and I anxiously hoped that something would be done for my people that it might be avoided. But there was bad management somewhere or the difficulty that has taken place would have been avoided.

When it was ascertained that we would not be permitted to go to Washington, I resolved upon my course and again tried to recruit some braves from Keokuk's band to accompany me, but could not.

Conceiving that the peaceable disposition of Keokuk and his people had been in a great measure the cause of our having been driven from our village, I ascribed their present feelings to the same cause, and immediately went to work to recruit all my own band and making preparations to ascend Rock River, I made my encampment on the Mississippi, where Fort Madison had stood. I requested my people to rendezvous at that place, sending out soldiers to bring in the warriors and stationed my sentinels in a position to prevent any from moving off until all were ready.

My party having all come in and got ready, we commenced our march up the Mississippi (36) ; our women and children in canoes, carrying such provisions as we had, camp equipage, etc. My braves and warriors were on horseback, armed and equipped for defense. The prophet came down, joining us below Rock River, having called at Rock Island on his way down to consult the war chief, agent and trader, who, he said, used many arguments to dissuade him from going with us, requesting him to come and meet us and turn us back. They told him also there was a war chief on his way to Rock Island with a large body of soldiers.

The prophet said he would not listen to this talk, because no war chief would dare molest us so long as we were at peace. That we had a right to go where we pleased

7

peaceably, and advised me to say nothing to my braves and warriors until we encamped that night. We moved onward until we arrived at the place where General Gaines had made his encampment the year before, and encamped for the night. The prophet then addressed my braves and warriors. He told them to "follow us and act like braves and we have nothing to fear and much to gain. The American chief may come, but will not, dare not, interfere with us so long as we are peaceable. We are not yet ready to act otherwise. We must wait until we ascend Rock River and receive our reinforcements, and we will then be able to withstand any army."

That night the White Beaver, General Atkinson, with a party of soldiers passed up in a steamboat. Our party became alarmed, expecting to meet the soldiers at Rock River to prevent us from going up. On our arrival at its mouth we discovered that the steamboat had passed on.

I was fearful that the war chief had stationed his men on some high bluff or in some ravine, that we might be taken by surprise. Consequently, on entering Rock River we commenced beating our drums and singing, to show the Americans we were not afraid.

Having met with no opposition we moved up Rock River leisurely for some distance when we were overtaken by an express from White Beaver with an order for me to return with my band and recross the Mississippi again. I sent him word that I would not, not recognizing his right to make such a demand, as I was acting peaceably and intended to go to the prophet's village at his request, to make corn.

The express returned. We moved on and encamped some distance below the prophet's village. Here another express came from the White Beaver, threatening to pursue us and drive us back if we did not return peaceably. This message roused the spirit of my band and all were determined to remain with me and contest the ground with the war chief, should he come and attempt to drive us. We therefore directed the express to say to the war chief "if he wished to fight us he might come on." We were determined never to be driven, and equally so, not to make the first attack, our object being to act only on the defensive. This we conceived to be our right.

Soon after the express returned, Mr. Gratiot, sub-agent for the Winnebagoes, came to our encampment. He had no interpreter and was compelled to talk through his chiefs. They said the object of his mission was to persuade us to return. But they advised us to go on, assuring us that the further we went up Rock River the more friends we would meet, and our situation would be bettered. They were on our side and all of their people were our friends. We must not give up, but continue to ascend Rock River, on which, in a short time, we would receive reinforcements sufficiently strong to repulse any enemy. They said they would go down with their agent to ascertain the strength of the enemy and then return and give us the news. They had to use some stratagem to deceive their agent in order to help us.

During this council several of my braves hoisted the British flag, mounted their horses and surrounded the council lodge. I discovered that the agent was very much frightened. I told one of the chiefs to tell him that he need not be alarmed and then went out and directed my braves to desist. Every warrior immediately dismounted and returned to his lodge. After the council adjourned I placed a sentinel at the agent's lodge to guard him, fearing that some of my warriors might again frighten him. I had always thought he was a good man and was determined that he should not be hurt. He started with his chiefs to Rock Island.

Having ascertained that White Beaver would not permit us to remain where we were, I began to consider what was best to be done, and concluded to keep on up the river, see the Pottawattomies and have a talk with them. Several Winnebago chiefs were present, whom I advised of my intentions, as they did not seem disposed to render us any assistance. I asked them if they had not sent us wampum during the winter, and requested us to come and join their people and enjoy all the rights and privileges of their country. They did not deny this; and said if the white people did not interfere they had no objection to our making corn this year with our friend, the prophet, but did not wish us to go any further up.

The next day I started with my party to Kishwacokee. That night I encamped a short distance above the prophet's village. After all was quiet in our camp I sent for my chiefs and told them that we had been deceived. That all the fair promises that had been held out to us through Neapope were false. But it would not do to let our party know it. We must keep it secret among ourselves, move on to Kishwacokee, as if all was right, and say something on the way to encourage our people. I will then call on the Pottawattomies, hear what they say, and see what they will do.

We started the next morning after telling our people that news had just come from Milwaukee that a chief of our British Father would be there in a few days. Finding that all our plans were defeated, I told the prophet that he must go with me and we would see what could be done with the Pottawattomies. On our arrival at Kishwacokee an express was sent to the Pottawattomie villages. The next day a deputation arrived. I inquired if they had corn in their villages. They said they had very little and could not spare any. I asked them different questions and received very unsatisfactory answers. This talk was in the presence of all my people. I afterwards spoke to them privately and requested them to come to my lodge after my people had gone to sleep. They came and took seats. I asked them if they had received any news from the British on the lake. They said no. I inquired if they had heard that a chief of our British Father was coming to Milwaukee to bring us guns, ammunition, goods and provisions. They said no. I told them what news had been brought to me and requested them to return to their village and tell the chiefs that I wished to see them and have a talk with them.

After this deputation started I concluded to tell my people that if White Beaver came after us we would go back, as it was useless to think of stopping or going on without more provisions and ammunition. I discovered that the Winnebagoes and Pottawattomies were not disposed to render us any assistance. The next day the Pottawattomie chiefs arrived in my camp. I had a dog killed and made a feast. When it was ready I spread my medicine bags and the chiefs began to eat. When the ceremony was about ending I received news that three or four hundred white men on horseback had been seen about eight miles off. I immediately started three young men with a white flag to meet them and conduct them to our camp, that we might hold a council with them and descend Rock River again. I also directed them, in case the whites had encamped, to return and I would go and see them. After this party had started I sent five young men to see what might take place. The first party went to the camp of the whites and were taken prisoners. The last party had not proceeded far before they saw about twenty men coming toward them at full gallop. They stopped, and, finding that the whites were coming toward them in such a warlike attitude, they turned and retreated, but were pursued and two of them overtaken and killed. The others made their escape. When they came in with the news I was preparing my flags to meet the war chief. The alarm was given. Nearly all my young men were absent ten miles away. I started with what I had left, about forty, and had proceeded but a short distance before we saw a part of the army approaching. I raised a yell, saying to my braves, "Some of our people have been killed. Wantonly and cruelly murdered! We must avenge their death!"

In a little while we discovered the whole army coming towards us at a full gallop. We were now confident that our first party had been killed. I immediately placed my men behind a cluster of bushes that we might have the first fire when they had approached close enough. They made a halt some distance from us. I gave another yell and ordered my brave warriors to charge upon them, expecting that they would all be killed. They did charge. Every man rushed towards the enemy and fired, and they retreated in the utmost confusion and consternation before my little but brave band of warriors.

After following the enemy some distance I found it useless to pursue them further as they rode so fast, and returned to the encampment with a few braves, as about twenty-five of them continued in pursuit of the flying enemy. I lighted my pipe and sat down to thank the Great Spirit for what he had done. I had not been meditating long when two of the three young men I had sent with the flag to meet the American war chief, entered. My astonishment was not greater than my joy to see them living and well. I eagerly listened to their story, which was as follows:

"When we arrived near the encampment of the whites a number of them rushed out to meet us, bringing their guns with them. They took us into their camp, where an American who spoke the Sac language a little, told us that his chief wanted to know who we were, where we were going, where our camp was, and where was Black Hawk? He told him that we had come to see his chief, that our chief had

BLACK HAWK'S AUTOBIOGRAPHY   103

directed us to conduct him to our camp in case he had not encamped, and in that event to tell him that he, Black Hawk, would come to see him; he wished to hold a council with him, as he had given up all intention of going to war."

This man had once been a member of our tribe (37), having been adopted by me many years before and treated with the same kindness as was shown to our young men, but like the caged bird of the woods, he yearned for freedom, and after a few years' residence with us an opportunity for escape came and he left us. On this occasion he would have respected our flag and carried back the message I had sent to his chief, had he not been taken prisoner with a comrade, by some of my braves who did not recognize him, and brought him into camp. They were securely tied with cords to trees and left to meditate, but were occasionally buffeted by my young men when passing near them. When I passed by him there was a recognition on the part of us both, but on account of former friendship I concluded to let him go, and some little time before the sun went down I released him from his captivity by untying the cords that bound him and accompanied him outside of our lines so that he could escape safely. His companion had previously made a desperate effort to escape from his guards and was killed by them.

They continued their story:

"At the conclusion of this talk a party of white men came in on horseback. We saw by their countenances that something had happened. A general tumult arose. They looked at us with indignation, talked among themselves for a moment, when several of them cocked their guns and fired at us in the crowd. Our companion fell dead. We rushed through the crowd and made our escape. We remained in ambush but a short time before we heard yelling like Indians running an enemy. In a little while we saw some of the whites in full speed. One of them came near us. I threw my tomahawk and struck him on the head, which brought him to the ground; I ran to him and with his own knife took off his scalp. I took his gun, mounted his horse, and brought my friend here behind me. We turned to follow our braves, who were chasing the enemy, and had not gone far before we overtook a white man whose horse had mired in a swamp. My friend alighted and tomahawked the man, who was apparently fast under his horse. He took his scalp, horse and gun. By this time our party was some distance ahead. We followed on several miles and met our party returning. We asked them how many of our men had been killed. We inquired how many whites had been killed. They replied that they did not know, but said we will soon ascertain as we must scalp them as we go back. On our return we found ten men besides the two we had killed before we joined our friends. Seeing that they did not yet recognize us, it being dark, we again asked how many of our braves had been killed. They said five. We asked who they were? They replied that the first party of three who went out to meet the American war chief had all been taken prisoners and killed in the encampment, and that out of a party of five, who followed to see the meeting of the first party with the whites, two had been killed. We were now certain that they did not recognize us, nor did we tell who we were until we arrived at our camp. The news of our death had reached it some time before and all were surprised to see us again."

The next morning I told the crier of my village to give notice that we must go and bury our dead. In a little while all were ready. A small deputation was sent for our absent warriors and the remainder started to bury the dead. We first disposed of them and then commenced an examination in the enemy's deserted encampment for plunder. We found arms and ammunition and provisions, all of which we were sadly in want of, particularly the latter, as we were entirely without. We found also a variety of saddle-bags, which I distributed among my braves, a small quantity of whisky and some little barrels that had contained this bad medicine but they were empty. I was surprised to find that the whites carried whisky with them, as I had understood that all the palefaces, when acting as soldiers in the field, were strictly temperate.

The enemy's encampment was in a skirt of woods near a run, about half a day's travel from Dixon's ferry. We attacked them in the prairie, with a few bushes between us, about sundown, and I expected that my whole party would be killed. I never was so much surprised in all the fighting I have seen, knowing, too, that the Americans generally shoot well, as I was to see this army of several hundred retreating, without showing fight; and passing immediately through their encampment, I did think they intended to halt there, as the situation would have forbidden attack by my party if their number had not exceeded half of mine, as we would have been compelled to take the open prairie whilst they could have picked trees to shield themselves from our fire.

I was never so much surprised in my life as I was in this attack. An army of three or four hundred men, after having learned that we were suing for peace, to attempt to kill the flag bearers that had gone unarmed to ask for a meeting of the war chiefs of the two contending parties to hold a council, that I might return to the west side of the Mississippi, to come forward with a full determination to demolish the few braves I had with me, to retreat when they had ten to one, was unaccountable to me. It proved a different spirit from any I had ever before seen among the palefaces. I expected to see them fight as the Americans did with the British during the last war, but they had no such braves among them.

At our feast with the Pottawattomies I was convinced that we had been imposed upon by those who had brought in reports of larger reinforcements to my band and resolved not to strike a blow; and in order to get permission from White Beaver to return and re-cross the Mississippi, I sent a flag of peace to the American war chief, who was reported to be close by with his army, expecting that he would convene a council and listen to what we had to say. But this chief, instead of pursuing that honorable and chivalric course, such as I have always practiced, shot down our flag bearer and thus forced us into war with less than five hundred warriors to contend against three or four thousand soldiers.

The supplies that Neapope and the prophet told us about, and the reinforcements we were to have, were never more heard of; and it is but justice to our British Father to say were never promised, his chief having sent word in lieu of the lies that were brought to me, "for us to remain at peace as we could accomplish nothing but our own ruin by going to war."

What was now to be done? It was worse than folly to turn back and meet an enemy where the odds were so much against us and thereby sacrifice ourselves, our wives and children to the fury of an enemy who had murdered some of our brave and unarmed warriors when they were on a mission to sue for peace.

Having returned to our encampment and found that all our young men had come in, I sent out spies to watch the movements of the army, and commenced moving up Kishwacokee with the balance of my people. I did not know where to go to find a place of safety for my women and children, but expected to find a good refuge about the head of Rock River. I concluded to go there and thought my best route would be to go round the head of Kishwacokee, so that the Americans would have some difficulty if they attempted to follow us.

CHAPTER XII.

BLACK HAWK'S FLIGHT TOWARD THE FOUR LAKES—
SEVERAL ENCOUNTERS—MASSACRE OF THE DAVIS AND
HALL FAMILIES—BATTLE AT WISCONSIN HEIGHTS—
FLIGHT TOWARD THE MISSISSIPPI—MASSACRE AT THE
BAD AXE.

On arriving at the head of Kishwacokee, I was met by a party of Winnebagoes, who seemed to rejoice at our success. They said they had come to offer their services and were anxious to join us. I asked them if they knew where there was a safe place for our women and children. They told us that they would send two old men with us to guide us to a good safe place.

I arranged war parties to send out in different directions before I proceeded further. The Winnebagoes went alone. The war parties having all been fitted out and started we commenced moving to the Four Lakes, the place where our guides were to conduct us. We had not gone far before six Winnebagoes came in with one scalp. They said they had killed a man at a grove on the road from Dixon's to the lead mines. Four days after the party of Winnebagoes who had gone out from the head of Kishwacokee overtook us, and told me that they had killed four men and taken their scalps; and that one of them was Keokuk's father (the agent). They proposed to have a dance over their scalps. I told them that I could have no dancing in my camp, in consequence of my having lost three young braves; but they might dance in their own camp, which they did. Two days after we arrived in safety at the place where the Winnebagoes had directed us. In a few days a great number of our warriors came in. I called them all around me and addressed them. I told them:

"Now is the time, if any of you wish to come into distinction and be honored with the medicine bag! Now is the time to show your courage and bravery, and avenge the murder of our three braves!"

Several small parties went out and returned again in a few days with success, bringing in provisions for our people. In the meantime, some spies came in and reported that the army had fallen back to Dixon's ferry; and others brought news that the horsemen had broken up their camp, disbanded, and returned home.

Finding that all was safe, I made a dog feast, preparatory to leaving my camp with a large party (as the enemy were stationed so far off). Before my braves commenced feasting I took my medicine bags and addressed them in the following language:

"Braves and warriors: These are the medicine bags of our forefather, Mukataquet, who was the father of the Sac nation. They were handed down to the great war chief of our nation, Nanamakee, who has been at war with all the nations of the plains and have never yet been disgraced! I expect you all to protect them!"

After the ceremony was over and our feasting done, I started with about two hundred warriors following my great medicine bags. I directed my course toward sunset, and dreamed, the second night after we started, that there would be a great feast prepared for us after one day's travel. I told my warriors my dream in the morning and we started for Mosochocoynak (Apple River). When we arrived in the vicinity of a fort the white people had built, we saw four men on horseback. One of my braves fired and wounded a man, when the others set up a yell as if a large force were near and ready to come against us. We concealed ourselves and remained in this position for some time, watching to see the enemy approach, but none came. The four men, in the meantime, ran to the fort and gave

BLACK HAWK'S AUTOBIOGRAPHY   109

the alarm. We followed them and attacked the fort. One of their braves, who seemed more valiant than the rest, raised his head above the picketing to fire at us when one of my braves, with a well-directed shot, put an end to his bravery. Finding that these people could not be killed without setting fire to their houses and fort I thought it more prudent to be content with what flour, provisions, cattle and horses we could find than to set fire to their buildings, as the light would be seen at a distance and the army might suppose we were in the neighborhood and come upon us with a strong force. Accordingly, we opened a house and filled our bags with flour and provisions, took several horses and drove off some of their cattle.

We started in a direction toward sunrise. After marching a considerable time I discovered some white men coming towards us. I told my braves that we would go into the woods and kill them when they approached. We concealed ourselves until they came near enough and then commenced yelling and firing, and made a rush upon them. About this time their chief, with a party of men, rushed up to rescue the men we had fired upon. In a little while they commenced retreating and left their chief and a few braves who seemed willing and anxious to fight. They acted like men, but were forced to give way when I rushed upon them with my braves. In a short time the chief returned with a larger party. He seemed determined to fight and anxious for a battle. When he came near enough I raised the yell and firing commenced from both sides. The chief, who seemed to be a small man, addressed his warriors in a loud voice, but they soon retreated, leaving him and a few braves on the battlefield. A great number of my warriors pursued the retreating party and killed a number of their horses as they ran. The chief and his few braves were unwilling to leave the field. I ordered my braves to rush upon them and had the mortification of seeing two of my chiefs killed before the enemy retreated.

This young chief deserves great praise for his courage and bravery, but fortunately for us, his army was not all composed of such brave men.

During this attack we killed several men and about forty horses, and lost two young chiefs and seven warriors. My braves were anxious to pursue them to the fort, attack and burn it, but I told them it was useless to waste our powder as there was no possible chance of success if we did attack them, and that as we had run the bear into his hole we would there leave him and return to our camp.

On arriving at our encampment we found that several of our spies had returned, bringing intelligence that the army had commenced moving. Another party of five came in and said they had been pursued for several hours, and were attacked by twenty-five or thirty whites in the woods; that the whites rushed in upon them as they lay concealed and received their fire without seeing them. They immediately retreated whilst we reloaded. They entered the thicket again and as soon as they came they rushed into the thicket and fired. We returned their fire and a skirmish ensued between two of their men and one of ours, who was killed by having his throat cut. This was the only man we lost, the enemy having had three killed; they again retreated.

Another party of three Sacs had come in and brought two young white squaws, whom they had given to the Winnebagoes to take to the whites. They said they had joined a party of Pottawattomies and went with them as a war party against the settlers of Illinois.

The leader of this party, a Pottawattomie, had been severely whipped by this settler some time before, and was anxious to avenge the insult and injury. While the party was preparing to start, a young Pottawattomie went to the settler's home and told him to leave it, that a war party was coming to murder them. They started, but soon returned again, as it appeared that they were all there when the war party arrived. The Pottawattomies killed the whole family except two young white squaws (38), whom the Sacs took up on their horses and carried off to save their lives. They were brought to our encampment and a messenger sent to the Winnebagoes, as they were friendly on both sides, to come and get them and carry them to the whites. If these young men, belonging to my band, had not gone with the Pottawattomies, the two young squaws would have shared the same fate as their friends.

During our encampment at the Four Lakes we were hard pressed to obtain enough to eat to support nature. Situated in a swampy, marshy country (which had been selected in consequence of the great difficulty required to gain access thereto), there was but little game of any sort to be found, and fish were equally scarce. The great distance to any settlement, and the impossibility of bringing supplies therefrom, if any could have been obtained, deterred our young men from making further attempts. We were forced to dig roots and bark trees to obtain something to satisfy hunger and keep us alive. Several of our old people became so reduced as to actually die with hunger! Learning that the army had commenced moving and fearing that they might come upon and surround our encampment, I concluded to remove our women and children across the Mississippi, that they might return to the Sac nation again. Accordingly, on the next day we commenced moving, with five Winnebagoes acting as our guides, intending to descend the Wisconsin.

Neapope, with a party of twenty, remained in our rear to watch for the enemy, whilst we were proceeding to the Wisconsin, with our women and children. We arrived, and had commenced crossing over to an island, when we discovered a large body of the enemy coming towards us. We were now compelled to fight, or sacrifice our wives and children to the fury of the whites. I met them with fifty warriors (having left the balance to assist our women and children in crossing), about a mile from the river, on a fine horse, and was pleased to see my warriors so brave. I addressed them in a loud voice, telling them to stand their ground and never yield it to the enemy. At this time I was on the rise of a hill (Wisconsin Heights, at Prairie du Sac), where I wished to form my warriors, that we might have some advantage over the whites. But the enemy succeeded in gaining this point, which compelled us to fall into a deep ravine, from which we continued firing at them and they at us, until it began to grow dark. My horse having been wounded twice during this engagement, and fearing from his loss of blood that he would soon give out, and finding that the enemy would not come near enough to receive our fire in the dusk of the evening, and knowing that our women and children had had sufficient time to reach the island in the Wisconsin, I ordered my warriors to return by different routes and meet me at the Wisconsin, and was astonished to find that the enemy were not disposed to pursue us.

In this skirmish with fifty braves I defended and accomplished my passage over the Wisconsin with a loss of only six men, though opposed by a host of mounted militia. I would not have fought there but to gain time for our women and children to cross to an island. A warrior will duly appreciate the embarrassments I labored under—and whatever may be the sentiments of the white people in relation to this battle, my nation, though fallen, will award to me the reputation of a great brave in conducting it.

The loss of the enemy could not be ascertained by our party; but I am of the opinion that it was much greater, in proportion, than mine. We returned to the Wisconsin and crossed over to our people.

Here some of my people left me and descended the

Wisconsin, hoping to escape to the west side of the Mississippi, that they might return home. I had no objection to them leaving me, as my people were all in a desperate condition, being worn out with traveling and starving with hunger. Our only hope to save ourselves was to get across the Mississippi. But few of this party escaped. Unfortunately for them, a party of soldiers from Prairie du Chien were stationed on the Wisconsin, a short distance from its mouth, who fired upon our distressed people. Some were killed, others drowned, several taken prisoners, and the balance escaped to the woods and perished with hunger. Among this party were a great many women and children.

I was astonished to find that Neapope and his party of spies had not yet come in, they having been left in my rear to bring the news if the enemy were discovered. It appeared, however, that the whites had come in a different direction and intercepted our trail but a short distance from the place where we first saw them, leaving our spies considerably in the rear. Neapope and one other retired to the Winnebago village, and there remained during the war. The balance of his party, being brave men, and considering our interests as their own, returned and joined our ranks.

Myself and band having no means to descend the Wisconsin, I started over a rugged country to go to the Mississippi, intending to cross it and return to my nation. Many of our people were compelled to go on foot for want of horses, which, in consequence of their having had nothing to eat for a long time, caused our march to be very slow. At length we arrived at the Mississippi, having lost some of our old men and children, who perished on the way with hunger.

We had been here but a little while before we saw a steamboat (the "Warrior") coming. I told my braves not to shoot, as I intended going on board, so that we might save our women and children. I knew the captain (Trockmorton) and was determined to give myself up to him. I then sent for my white flag. While the messenger was gone I took a small piece of white cotton and put it on a pole and called to the captain of the boat and told him to send his little canoe ashore and let me come aboard. The people on board asked whether we were Sacs or Winnebagoes. I told a Winnebago to tell them that we were Sacs and wanted to give ourselves up! A Winnebago on the boat called out to us "to run and hide, that the whites were going to shoot!" About this time one of my braves had jumped into the river, bearing a white flag to the boat, when another sprang in after him and brought him to the shore. The firing then commenced from the boat, which was returned by my braves and continued for some time. Very few of my people were hurt after the first fire, having succeeded in getting behind old logs and trees, which shielded them from the enemy's fire.

The Winnebago on the steamboat must either have misunderstood what was told, or did not tell it to the captain correctly, because I am confident he would not have allowed the soldiers to fire upon us if he had known my wishes. I have always considered him a good man and too great a brave to fire upon an enemy when suing for quarter.

After the boat left us, I told my people to cross if they could and wished; that I intended going into the Chippewa country. Some commenced crossing, and such as had determined to follow them, remained; only three lodges going with me. Next morning at daybreak a young man overtook me, and said that all my party had determined to cross the Mississippi—that a number had already got over safe, and that he had heard the white army last night within a few miles of them. I now began to fear that the whites would come up with my people and kill them before they could get across. I had determined to go and join the

BLACK HAWK'S AUTOBIOGRAPHY 115

Chippewas; but reflecting that by this I could only save myself, I concluded to return and die with my people, if the Great Spirit would not give us another victory. During our stay in the thicket a party of whites came close by us, but passed on without discovering us.

Early in the morning a party of whites, being in advance of the army, came upon our people, who were attempting to cross the Mississippi. They tried to give themselves up; the whites paid no attention to their entreaties, but commenced slaughtering them. In a little while the whole army arrived. Our braves, but few in number, finding that the enemy paid no regard to age or sex, and seeing that they were murdering helpless women and little children, determined to fight until they were killed. As many women as could commenced swimming the Mississippi with their children on their backs; a number of them were drowned, and some shot before they could reach the opposite shore.

One of my braves, who gave me this information, piled up some saddles before him (when the fight commenced), to shield himself from the enemy's fire, and killed three white men. But seeing that the whites were coming too close to him, he crawled to the bank of the river without being perceived, and hid himself under the bank until the enemy retired. He then came to me and told me what had been done. After hearing this sorrowful news I started with my little party to the Winnebago village at Prairie La Cross. On my arrival there I entered the lodge of one of the chiefs, and told him that I wished him to go with me to his father, that I intended giving myself up to the American war chief and die, if the Great Spirit saw proper. He said he would go with me. I then took my medicine bag and addressed the chief. I told him that it was "the soul of the Sac nation—that it never had been dishonored in any battle, take it, it is my life—dearer than life—and give it to the American chief!" He said he would keep it, and take care of it, and if I was suffered to live he would send it to me.

During my stay at the village the squaws made me a white dress of deer skin. I then started with several Winnebagoes and went to their agent [Gen. J. M. Street], at Prairie du Chien, and gave myself up.

On my arrival there, I found to my sorrow that a large body of Sioux had pursued and killed a number of our women and children, who had got safely across the Mississippi. The whites ought not to have permitted such conduct, and none but cowards would ever have been guilty of such cruelty, a habit which has always been practiced on our nation by the Sioux.

The massacre, which terminated the war, lasted about two hours. Our loss in killed was about sixty, besides a number that were drowned. The loss of the enemy could not be ascertained by my braves, exactly; but they think that they killed about sixteen during the action.

CHAPTER XIII.

SURRENDER OF BLACK HAWK—PLACED IN CHARGE OF JEFFERSON DAVIS—IMPRISONMENT AT JEFFERSON BARRACKS—STARTS ON TOUR OF THE EASTERN STATES—SURPRISED TO SEE THE RAILROADS—INTERVIEW WITH PRESIDENT JACKSON—AT FORTRESS MONROE—VISITS MANY CITIES—HIS IMPRESSIONS.

I was now given up by the agent of the commanding officer at Fort Crawford, the White Beaver having gone down the river. We remained here a short time, and then started for Jefferson Barracks, in a steamboat, under the charge of a young chief (Lieut. Jefferson Davis), who treated us all with much kindness. He is a good and brave young chief, with whose conduct I was much pleased. On our way down we called at Galena and remained a short time. The people crowded to the boat to see us; but the war chief would not permit them to enter the apartment where we were—knowing, from what his feelings would have been if he had been placed in a similar situation, that we did not wish to have a gaping crowd around us.

We passed Rock Island without stopping. The great war chief, General Scott, who was then at Fort Armstrong, came out in a small boat to see us, but the captain of the steamboat would not allow anybody from the fort to come on board his boat, in consequence of the cholera raging among the soldiers. I did think that the captain ought to have permitted the war chief to come on board to see me, because I could see no danger to be apprehended by it. The war chief looked well, and I have since heard was constantly among his soldiers, who were sick and dying, administering to their wants, and had not caught the disease from them, and I thought it absurd to think that any of the people on the steamboat could be afraid of catching the disease from a well man. But these people are not brave like war chiefs, who never fear anything.

On our way down I surveyed the country that had cost us so much trouble, anxiety and blood, and that now caused me to be a prisoner of war. I reflected upon the ingratitude of the whites when I saw their fine houses, rich harvest and everything desirable around them; and recollected that all this land had been ours, for which I and my people had never received a dollar, and that the whites were not satisfied until they took our village and our graveyards from us and removed us across the Mississippi.

On our arrival at Jefferson Barracks we met the great war chief, White Beaver, who had commanded the American army against my little band. I felt the humiliation of my situation; a little while before I had been leader of my braves, now I was a prisoner of war, but had surrendered myself. He received us kindly and treated us well.

We were now confined to the barracks and forced to wear the ball and chain. This was extremely mortifying and altogether useless. Was the White Beaver afraid I would break out of his barracks and run away? Or was he ordered to inflict this punishment upon me? If I had taken him prisoner on the field of battle I would not have wounded his feelings so much by such treatment, knowing that a brave war chief would prefer death to dishonor. But I do not blame the White Beaver for the course he pursued, as it is the custom among the white soldiers, and I suppose was a part of his duty.

The time dragged heavily and gloomily throughout the winter, although the White Beaver did everything in his power to render us comfortable. Having been accustomed, throughout a long life, to roam the forests, to go and come at liberty, confinement, and under such circumstances, could not be less than torture.

We passed away the time making pipes until spring, when we were visited by the agent, trader and interpreter, from Rock Island, Keokuk and several chiefs and braves of our nation, and my wife and daughter. I was rejoiced to see the two latter and spent my time very agreeably with them and my people as long as they remained.

The trader, Sagenash (Colonel Davenport) presented me with some dried venison, which had been killed and cured by some of my friends. This was a valuable present, and although he had given me many before, none ever pleased me so much. This was the first meat I had eaten for a long time that reminded me of the former pleasures of my own wigwam, which had always been stored with plenty.

Keokuk and his chiefs, during their stay at the barracks, petitioned our Great Father, the president, to release us, and pledged themselves for our good conduct. I now began to hope I would soon be restored to liberty and the enjoyment of my family and friends, having heard that Keokuk stood high in the estimation of our Great Father, because he did not join in the war, but I was soon disappointed in my hopes. An order came from our Great Father to the White Beaver to send us to Washington.

In a little while all were ready and left Jefferson Barracks on board of a steamboat, under charge of a young war chief and one soldier, whom the White Beaver sent along as a guide to Washington. We were accompanied by Keokuk, wife and son, Appanooce, Wapello, Poweshiek, Pashippaho, Nashashuk, Saukee, Musquaukee, and our interpreter. Our principal traders, Col. George Davenport, of Rock Island, and S. S. Phelps and clerk, William Courland, of the Yellow Banks, also accompanied us. On our way up the Ohio we passed several large villages, the names of which were explained to me. The first is called Louisville, and is a very pretty village, situated on the bank of the Ohio river. The next is Cincinnati, which stands on the bank of the same river. This is a large and beautiful village and seemed to be in a thriving condition. The people gathered on the banks as we passed, in great crowds, apparently anxious to see us.

On our arrival at Wheeling the streets and river banks were crowded with people, who flocked from every direction to see us. While we remained here many called upon us and treated us with kindness, no one offering to molest or misuse us. This village is not so large as either of those before mentioned, but is quite a pretty village.

We left the steamboat here, having traveled a long distance on the prettiest river I ever saw (except our Mississippi) and took the stage. Being unaccustomed to this mode of traveling, we soon got tired and wished ourselves seated in a canoe on one of our own rivers, that we might return to our friends. We had traveled but a short distance before our carriage turned over, from which I received a slight injury, and the soldier had one arm broken. I was sorry for this accident, as the young man had behaved well.

We had a rough and mountainous country for several days, but had a good trail for our carriage. It is astonishing what labor and pains the white people have had to make this road, as it passes over several mountains, which are generally covered with rocks and timbers, yet it has been made smooth and easy to travel upon.

Rough and mountainous as this country is there are many wigwams and small villages standing on the roadside. I could see nothing in the country to induce the people to live in it, and was astonished to find so many whites living on the hills.

I have often thought of them since my return to my own people, and am happy to think that they prefer living in their own country to coming out to ours and driving us from it, as many of the whites have already done. I think with them, that wherever the Great Spirit places his people they ought to be satisfied to remain, and be thankful for what He has given them, and not drive others from the country He has given them because it happens to be better than theirs. This is contrary to our way of thinking, and from my intercourse with the whites, I have learned that one great principle of their religion is "to do unto others as you wish them to do unto you." Those people in the mountains seem to act upon this principle, but the settlers on our frontiers and on our lands seem never to think of it, if we are to judge by their actions.

The first village of importance that we came to, after leaving the mountains, is called Hagerstown. It is a large village to be so far from a river and is very pretty. The people appear to live well and enjoy themselves much.

We passed through several small villages on the way to Fredericktown, but I have forgotten their names. This last is a large and beautiful village. The people treated us well, as they did at all other villages where we stopped.

Here we came to another road much more wonderful than that through the mountains. They call it a railroad (the Baltimore and Ohio). I examined it carefully, but need not describe it, as the whites know all about it. The great road over the mountains will bear no comparison to it, although it has given the white people much trouble to make. I was surprised to see so much money and labor expended to make a good road for easy traveling. I prefer riding horseback, however, to any other way, but suppose these people would not have gone to so much trouble and expense to make a road if they did not prefer riding in their new fashioned carriages, which seem to run without any trouble, being propelled by steam on the same principle that boats are on the river. They certainly deserve great praise for their industry.

On our arrival at Washington, we called to see our Great Father, the president. He looks as if he had seen as many winters as I have, and seems to be a great brave. I had very little talk with him, as he appeared to be busy and did not seem to be much disposed to talk. I think he is a good man; and although he talked but little, he treated us very well. His wigwam is well furnished with every thing good and pretty, and is very strongly built.

He said he wished to know the cause of my going to war against his white children. I thought he ought to have known this before; and consequently said but little to him about it, as I suspected he knew as well as I could tell him.

He said he wanted us to go to Fortress Monroe and stay awhile with the war chief who commanded it. But having been so long from my people, I told him I would rather return to my nation; that Keokuk had come here once on a visit to him, as we had done, and he had let him return again, as soon as he wished, and that I expected to be treated in the same manner. He insisted, however, on our going to Fortress Monroe; and as the interpreter then present could not understand enough of our language to interpret a speech, I concluded it was best to obey our Great Father, and say nothing contrary to his wishes.

During our stay at the city, we were called upon by many of the people, who treated us well, particularly the squaws; we visited the great council house of the Americans; the place where they keep their big guns; and all the public buildings, and then started for Fortress Monroe. The war chief met us on our arrival, and shook hands, and appeared glad to see me. He treated us with great friendship, and talked to me frequently. Previous to our leaving this fort, he made us a feast, and gave us some presents, which I intend to keep for his sake. He is a very good man and a great brave. I was sorry to leave him, although I was going to return to my people, because he had treated me like a brother, during all the time I remained with him.

Having got a new guide, a war chief (Major Garland), we started for our own country, taking a circuitous route. Our Great Father being about to pay a visit to his children in the big towns toward sunrise, and being desirous that we should have an opportunity of seeing them, had directed our guide to take us through.

On our arrival at Baltimore, we were much astonished to see so large a village; but the war chief told us we would soon see a larger one. This surprised us more. During our stay here, we visited all the public buildings and places of amusement, saw much to admire, and were well entertained by the people who crowded to see us. Our Great Father was there at the same time, and seemed to be much liked by his white children, who flocked around him (as they had around us) to shake him by the hand. He did not remain long, having left the city before us. In an interview while here, the President said:

"When I saw you in Washington, I told you that you had behaved very badly in going to war against the whites. Your conduct then compelled me to send my warriors against you, and your people were defeated with great loss, and several of you surrendered, to be kept until I should be satisfied that you would not try to do any more injury. I told you, too, that I would inquire whether your people wished you to return, and whether, if you did return, there would be any danger to the frontier. General Clark and General Atkinson, whom you know, have informed me that your principal chief and the rest of your people are anxious you should return and Keokuk has asked me to send you back. Your chiefs have pledged themselves for your good conduct, and I have given directions that you should be taken to your own country.

"Major Garland, who is with you, will conduct you through some of our towns. You will see the strength of the white people. You will see that our young men are as numerous as the leaves in the wood. What can you do against us? You may kill a few women and children, but such a force would soon be sent against you as would destroy your whole tribe. Let the red men hunt and take care of their families. I hope they will not again raise the tomahawk against their white brethren. We do not wish to injure you. We desire your prosperity and improvement. But if you again make war against our people, I shall send a force which will severely punish you. When you go back, listen to the council of Keokuk and the other friendly chiefs; bury the tomahawk and live in peace with the people on the frontier. And I pray the Great Spirit to give you a smooth path and a fair sky to return."

I was pleased with our Great Father's talk and thanked him. Told him that the tomahawk had been buried so deep that it would never be resurrected, and that my remaining days would be spent in peace with all my white brethren.

We left Baltimore in a steamboat, and traveled in this way to the big village, where they make medals and money (Philadelphia). We again expressed surprise at finding this village so much larger than the one we had left; but the war chief again told us we would see another much larger than this. I had no idea that the white people had such large villages, and so many people. They were very kind to us, showed us all their great public works, their ships and steamboats. We visited the place where they make money (the mint) and saw the men engaged in it. They presented each of us with a number of pieces of the coin as they fell from the mint, which are very handsome.

I witnessed a militia training in this city, in which were performed a number of singular military feats. The chiefs and men were all well dressed, and exhibited quite a warlike appearance. I think our system of military parade far better than that of the whites, but as I am now done going to war I will not describe it, or say anything more about war, or the preparations necessary for it.

We next started for New York, and on our arrival near the wharf, saw a large collection of people gathered at Castle Garden. We had seen many wonderful sights in our way—large villages, the great national road over the mountains, the railroad, steam carriages, ships, steamboats and many other things; but we were now about to witness a sight more surprising than any of these. We were told that a man was going up in the air in a balloon. We watched with anxiety to see if this could be true; and to our utter astonishment, saw him ascend in the air until the eye could no longer perceive him. Our people were all surprised and one of our young men asked the prophet if he was going up to see the Great Spirit?

After the ascension of the balloon, we landed and got into a carriage to go to the house that had been provided for our reception. We had proceeded but a short distance before the street was so crowded that it was impossible for the carriage to pass. The war chief then directed the coachman to take another street, and stop at a different house from the one we had intended. On our arrival here we were waited upon by a number of gentlemen, who seemed much pleased to see us. We were furnished with good rooms, good provisions, and everything necessary for our comfort.

The chiefs of this big village, being desirous that all their people should have an opportunity to see us, fitted up their great council house for this purpose, where we saw an immense number of people; all of whom treated us with great friendship, and many with great generosity. One of their great chiefs, John A. Graham, waited upon us and made a very pretty talk, which appeared in the village papers, one of which I now hand you:

"Brothers: Open your ears. You are brave men. You have fought like tigers, but in a bad cause. We have conquered you. We were sorry last year that you raised the tomahawk against us; but we believe you did not know us then as you do now. We think, in time to come, you will be wise, and that we shall be friends forever. You see that we are a great people, numerous as the flowers of the field, as the shells on the seashore, or the fishes in the sea. We put one hand on the eastern and at the same time the other on the western ocean. We all act together. If some time our great men talk long and loud at our council fires, but shed one drop of white man's blood, our young warriors, as thick as the stars of the night, will leap on board of our great boats, which fly on the waves and over the lakes—swift as the eagle in the air—then penetrate the woods, make the big guns thunder, and the whole heavens red with the flames of the dwellings of their enemies. Brothers, the President has made you a great talk. He has but one mouth. That one has sounded the sentiments of all the people. Listen to what he has said to you. Write it on your memories, it is good, very good.

"Black Hawk, take these jewels, a pair of topaz earrings, beautifully set in gold, for your wife or daughter, as a token of friendship, keeping always in mind that women and children are the favorites of the Great Spirit. These jewels are from an old man, whose head is whitened with the snows of seventy winters, an old man who has thrown down his bow, put off his sword, and now stands leaning on his staff, waiting the commands of the Great Spirit. Look around you, see all this mighty people, then go to your homes, open your arms to receive your families. Tell them to bury the hatchet, to make bright the chain of friendship, to love the white men and to live in peace with them, as long as the rivers run into the sea, and the sun rises and sets. If you do so, you will be happy. You will then insure the prosperity of unborn generations of your tribes, who will go hand in hand with the sons of the white men, and all shall be blessed by the Great Spirit. Peace and happiness by the blessing of the Great Spirit attend you. Farewell."

In reply to this fine talk, I said, "Brother: We like your talk. We like the white people. They are very kind to us. We shall not forget it. Your counsel is good. We shall attend to it. Your valuable present shall go to my squaw. We shall always be friends."

The chiefs were particular in showing us everything that they thought would be pleasing or gratifying to us. We went with them to Castle Garden to see the fire-works, which was quite an agreeable entertainment, but to the whites who witnessed it, less magnificent than would have been the sight of one of our large prairies when on fire.

We visited at the public buildings and places of amusement, which, to us, were truly astonishing yet very gratifying.

Everybody treated us with friendship, and many with great liberality. The squaws presented us many handsome little presents that are said to be valuable. They were very kind, very good, and very pretty—for palefaces.

Among the men, who treated us with marked friendship, by the presentation of many valuable presents, I cannot omit to mention the name of my old friend Crooks, of the American Fur Company. I have known him long, and have always found him to be a good chief, one who gives good advice, and treats our people right. I shall always be proud to recognize him as a friend, and glad to shake him by the hand.

BIRD'S-EYE VIEW OF ROCK ISLAND ARSENAL.

CHAPTER XIV.

RETURNS TO THE MISSISSIPPI—MEETS KEOKUK AT FORT ARMSTRONG—OFFENDED BY MAJOR GARLAND—HIS OPINION OF AMERICAN WAR CHIEFS—HOW HE WOULD HAVE SETTLED THE SLAVERY QUESTION—HIS FAREWELL WORDS TO THE AMERICANS.

Being anxious to return to our people, our guide started with us for our country. On arriving at Albany, the people were so anxious to see us, that they crowded the streets and wharves, where the steamboats landed, so much that it was almost impossible for us to pass to the hotel which had been provided for our reception. We remained here but a short time, it being a comparatively small village, with only a few large public buildings. The great council house of the state is located here, and the big chief (the governor) resides here, in an old mansion. From here we went to Buffalo, thence to Detroit, where I had spent many pleasant days, and anticipated, on my arrival, to meet many of my old friends, but in this I was disappointed. What could be the cause of this? Are they all dead? Or what has become of them? I did not see our old father there, who had always given me good advice and treated me with great friendship.

After leaving Detroit it was but a few days before we landed at Prairie du Chien. The war chief at the fort treated us very kindly, as did the people generally. I called on the agent of the Winnebagoes, (Gen. J. M. Street), to whom I had surrendered myself after the battle at Bad Axe, who received me very friendly. I told him that I had left my great medicine bag with his chiefs before I gave myself up; and now that I was to enjoy my liberty again, I was anxious to get it, that I might hand it down to my nation unsullied.

He said it was safe; he had heard his chiefs speak of it, and would get it and send it to me. I hope he will not forget his promise, as the whites generally do, because I have always heard that he was a good man, and a good father, and made no promise that he did not fulfill.

Passing down the Mississippi, I discovered a large collection of people in the mining country, on the west side of the river, and on the ground that we had given to our relation, Dubuqe, a long time ago. I was surprised at this, as I had understood from our Great Father that the Mississippi was to be the dividing line between his red and white children, and he did not wish either to cross it. I was much pleased with this talk, as I knew it would be much better for both parties. I have since found the country much settled by the whites further down and near to our people, on the west side of the river. I am very much afraid that in a few years they will begin to drive and abuse our people, as they have formerly done. I may not live to see it, but I feel certain the day is not far distant.

When we arrived at Rock Island, Keokuk and the other chiefs were sent for. They arrived the next day with a great number of their young men, and they all appeared glad to see me. Among them were some who had lost relations the year before. When we met, I perceived the tear of sorrow gush from their eyes, at the recollection of their loss, yet they exhibited a smiling countenance, from the joy they felt at seeing me alive and well.

The next morning, the war chief, our guide, convened a council at Fort Armstrong. Keokuk and his party went to the fort; but, in consequence of the war chief not having called for me to accompany him, I concluded that I would wait until I was sent for. Consequently, the interpreter came and said, "They are ready, and have been waiting for you to come to the fort." I told him I was ready and would accompany him. On our arrival there the council commenced. The war chief said that the object of this council was to deliver me up to Keokuk. He then read a paper, and directed me to follow Keokuk's advice, and be governed by his counsel in all things! In this speech he said much that was mortifying to my feelings, and I made an indignant reply.

I do not know what object the war chief had in making such a speech; or whether he intended what he said; but I do know that it was uncalled for, and did not become him. I have addressed many war chiefs and listened to their speeches with pleasure, but never had my feelings of pride and honor insulted on any other occasion. But I am sorry I was so hasty in reply to this chief, because I said that which I did not intend (39).

In this council I met my old friend (Col. Wm. Davenport), whom I had known about eighteen years. He is a good and brave chief. He always treated me well, and gave me good advice. He made me a speech on this occasion, very different from that of the other chief. It sounded like coming from a brave. He said he had known me a long time, that we had been good friends during that acquaintance, and, although he had fought against my braves, in our late war, he still extended the hand of friendship to me and hoped that I was now satisfied, from what I had seen in my travels, that it was folly to think of going to war against the whites, and would ever remain at peace. He said he would be glad to see me at all times, and on all occasions would be happy to give me good advice.

If our Great Father were to make such men our agents he would much better subserve the interests of our people, as well as his own, than in any other way. The war chiefs all know our people, and are respected by them. If the war chiefs at the different military posts on the frontier were made agents, they could always prevent difficulties from arising among the Indians and whites; and I have no doubt, had the war chief above alluded to been our agent, we would never have had the difficulties with the whites we have had. Our agents ought always to be braves. I would, therefore, recommend to our Great Father the propriety of breaking up the present Indian establishment, and creating a new one, and make the commanding officers at the different frontier posts the agents of the Government for the different nations of Indians.

I have a good opinion of the American war chiefs generally with whom I am acquainted, and my people, who had an opportunity of seeing and becoming well acquainted with the great war chief (Gen. Winfield Scott), who made the last treaty with them, in conjunction with the great chief of Illinois (Governor Reynolds), all tell me that he is the greatest brave they ever saw, and a good man—one who fulfills his promises. Our braves spoke more highly of him than of any chief that had ever been among us, or made treaties with us. Whatever he says may be depended upon. If he had been our Great Father we never would have been compelled to join the British in the last war with America, and I have thought that as our Great Father is changed every few years, that his children would do well to put this great war chief in his place, for they cannot find a better chief for a Great Father anywhere.

I would be glad if the village criers (editors), in all the villages I passed through, would let their people know my wishes and opinions about this great war chief.

During my travels my opinions were asked for on different subjects, but for want of a good interpreter (our regular interpreter having gone home on a different route), were seldom given. Presuming that they would be equally acceptable now, I have thought it a part of my duty to lay the most important before the public.

The subject of colonizing the negroes was introduced and my opinion asked as to the best method of getting clear of these people. I was not fully prepared at the time to answer, as I knew but little about their situation. I have since made many inquiries on the subject and find that a number of States admit no slaves, whilst the balance hold these negroes as slaves, and are anxious, but do not know how to get clear of them. I will now give my plan, which, when understood, I hope will be adopted.

Let the free States remove all the male negroes within their limits to the slave States; then let our Great Father buy all the female negroes in the slave States between the ages of twelve and twenty, and sell them to the people of the free States, for a term of years, say those under fifteen, for five years, and continue to buy all the females in the slave States as soon as they arrive at the age of twelve, and take them to the free States and dispose of them in the same way as the first, and it will not be long before the country is clear of the black skins, about which I am told they have been talking for a long time and for which they have expended a large amount of money.

I have no doubt but our Great Father would willingly do his part in accomplishing this object for his children, as he could not lose much by it, and would make them all happy. If the free States did not want them all for servants, we would take the balance in our nation to help our women make corn.

I have not time now, nor is it necessary to enter more into detail about my travels through the United States. The white people know all about them, and my people have started to their hunting grounds and I am anxious to follow them.

Before I take leave of the public, I must contradict the story of some of the village criers, who, I have been told, accuse me of having murdered women and children among the whites. This assertion is false. I never did nor have I any knowledge that any of my nation ever killed a white woman or child. I make this statement of truth to satisfy the white people among whom I have been traveling, and by whom I have been treated with great kindness, that, when they shook me by the hand so cordially, they did not shake the hand that had ever been raised against any but warriors.

It has always been our custom to receive all strangers that come to our village or camps in time of peace on terms of friendship, to share with them the best provisions we have, and give them all the assistance in our power. If on a journey or lost, to put them on the right trail, and if in want of moccasins, to supply them. I feel grateful to the whites for the kind manner they treated me and my party whilst traveling among them, and from my heart I assure them that the white man will always be welcome in our village or camps, as a brother. The tomahawk is buried forever! We will forget what has passed, and may the watchword between the Americans and the Sacs and Foxes ever be—"Friendship."

I am done now. A few more moons and I must follow my fathers to the shades. May the Great Spirit keep our people and the whites always at peace, is the sincere wish of

BLACK HAWK.

NOTES

CRITICAL AND HISTORICAL
By
JAMES D. RISHELL

1. "The Sac Village on Rock River." Pronounced *sauk* and not *sack*. In general, Indian names here have no accent. Thus, Keokuk, Wapello, Nam-e-qua, Py-e-sa, and the like, have only an apparent accent on the first syllable.

The name of the village was Sauk-e-nauk, or Saukenuk, as Catlin understood it; or Sauk-e-auk-e, as Judge Spencer understood Black Hawk to pronounce it in 1829. *Auk-e* is an Algonquin word, meaning place, land, or village. Thus, Milwaukee, or Minaukee, as the Indians called it, they having no *l* in their language, means "a good place or village." Algonac, in Michigan, as Schoolcraft points out, is Algon-auk, the place or town of the Algonquins. The word means, therefore, simply the Sauk village or place; just as we might call a place Frenchville or Germantown, according to the nationality of the settlers.

The Indian name of Rock River was Os-sin-i-sipi, or as it is frequently spelled, Assinnissippi. *Ossin* meant rock, or rocky, and *sipi* meant river. Thus, Ossinning, in New York, is compounded of *ossin,* rocky, and *ong* or *nong;* the latter syllable being identical in meaning with *au-ke.* The nasal *n* was a favorite sound with them, and seems sometimes to have been used and sometimes omitted. Other illustrations could be given, but these will be sufficient.

Os-sin-i-sipi meant, therefore, precisely what we call the stream—Rock River.

French maps of an early date, about 1680, show that the site of the village was then occupied by the Kickapoos, and the river was called the Kickapoo River. Within forty years thereafter, the Kickapoos had either abandoned the place or been driven from it. When the Sacs came here, probably not very far from 1725, it was in possession of the Kaskaskias, a tribe of the confederated Illini. These were driven out by the Sacs, as Black Hawk tells us.

In May, 1779, Spain declared war against Great Britain. A year later, Capt. Patrick Sinclair, in command of the British post at Mackinac, sent out an expedition of about 750 men, mostly Indians, for the purpose of co-operating with Gen. John Campbell in attacks upon the Spanish posts along the lower Mississippi. Captain Hesse was in command of the expedition, while Chief Wa-ba-sha led the Indian allies. A large part of Wa-ba-sha's force consisted of Sacs and Foxes who had joined him on the way south. Some conflict and obscurity in the evidence clouds the details of that adventure, but it is known that Wabasha's Indians started home after an unsuccessful attack upon St. Louis, pursued by Col. John Montgomery with a force of about 350 Americans and Spaniards, acting under orders from George Rogers Clark. He followed the retreating savages as far as the Rock River village, burning the crops and destroying the towns as he proceeded. At the Sac village, Colonel Montgomery was confronted by about 700 warriors; but their long and disastrous flight from St. Louis seems to have taken all the fight out of them, and they fled while Montgomery's men applied the torch to their village. Black Hawk was about 13 years old at the time of this occurrence. He makes no mention of it in his autobiography.

2. "The white man had arrived." This was probably Champlain; but whoever he was, he was quick to take advantage of the Indians' superstitious belief in dreams. He, too, had had a dream of like character, he said. He bound to himself the young Indian and his tribe by the ties of a common message from the Great Spirit.

3. "The son of the king of France." Of course this was a figure of speech. Father and children were terms in common use among the Indians to denote the relation of protection and allegiance.

4. "The British overpowered the French at Quebec." This tradition is entirely consistent with historical facts, and serves to limit the time of the departure of the Sacs from Canada. In 1629, Sir David Kirke, in an attempt to break up the French settlements in Canada, captured Quebec from Champlain. Three years later it was restored to the French. Neither before that time nor afterward did the British overpower the French and drive them away from Quebec, until the final surrender of that place to the British under Wolfe, in 1759. This entire paragraph seems to indicate that at a very early period, the Sacs had, in some way, been weaned from their former friendship for the French. Thus, we are told that it was to the "British Father" and not the French to whom they looked for supplies at Mackinac. It is a reasonable deduction that this was due to the influence of the Foxes, with whom they fell in soon after their arrival in the Lake country. See note 6.

5. "Different places along the lake." It is quite impossible to trace all the wanderings of this warlike and quarrelsome tribe in those Ishmaelitish days; but they left one striking memorial of a rather protracted stay in the word Sauk-e-nong, now called Saginaw, as applied to the city, river, and bay, in Michigan. See note 1. Some of the tribe were there as late as 1723, when they had a fight with their old friends, the Foxes, thus adding to the general turmoil of those days.

6. "The Foxes joined the Sacs." This alliance was most unfortunate for the Sacs, and was of no permanent benefit to the Foxes. Both tribes were Algonquins, but

BLACK HAWK'S AUTOBIOGRAPHY 137

the Foxes had been from time immemorial allies, and in some way, according to Parkman and others, kinsmen of the Iroquois. The Sacs, with their traditional friendship for Champlain and his people, would probably have got on very well with the French and their Indian friends in the new country; but the Foxes, wholly under the influence of their Iroquois kinsmen, shared the hatred of the latter against the French. Both tribes were therefore soon in deadly hostility to practically all of the other tribes in the Green Bay and Wisconsin region.

In the conflict known in our history as Queen Anne's War (1702-1713), the Iroquois had been induced to make a treaty of neutrality. This treaty was not very faithfully observed by the Indians. In the autumn of 1710, Iroquois messengers appeared at the Fox village near Green Bay, and induced the tribe to join in a war of extermination against the French. In the following spring, chiefs and warriors of the Fox nation with their women and children, in all about two thousand, appeared before the French fort at Detroit, and pitching their camp almost within its shadow, began to fortify it after the Indian fashion.

DuBuisson, who had succeeded Cadillac as commandant of the post, was greatly alarmed. He had only about thirty men, traders and coureur de bois, upon whom to depend for protection. His friendly Hurons and Ottawas had not yet returned from their annual hunt, and their wigwams were deserted. When DuBuisson inquired why they had come and why they were fortifying their camp with palisades, the Foxes replied that the land was their own and they would do as they pleased.

In response to messengers sent out by DuBuisson, the Hurons, Ottawas, Pottawattomies, and other friendly Indians came hurrying to the relief of the fort. The Foxes hastily withdrew into their camp and strengthened their intrenchments. The French allies were eager for the contest, but hesitated about making an assault upon so formidable a foe so strongly barricaded. But they kept up the siege, picking off the Foxes with their deadly rifles whenever one of them appeared. There was but little food in their camp and no water, and twice at least, the Foxes offered to surrender; But DuBuisson could give them no assurances of safety from the red allies who said they would be satisfied with nothing less than their extermination. For nineteen days the Foxes, dying with hunger and thirst, held resolutely to their post. Nor was the situation of the French much more favorable. The Foxes had been sending a rain of flaming arrows over the walls of the fort, kindling the thatched roofs of the buildings within the enclosure, thus destroying most of their ammunition and supplies. It was therefore determined that an assault should be made upon the intrenchments.

On a dark night, in the midst of a driving storm of wind and rain, the fierce Hurons and Ottawas, clambering over the palisades, sprang down with their dreadful warwhoop into the camp of the Foxes. But the wily foe, whether forewarned, or keenly interpreting the movements of the enemy, had fled.

On the following day the main body of the fugitives were overtaken, and then ensued one of the most merciless battles in the history of Indian warfare. All the Fox warriors, except the few who escaped in the confusion, were slain, or captured only to be reserved for the torture. The women and children were divided among the victors as slaves.

The remnant of the Foxes, still unsubdued, and crazed with the desire to avenge the terrible slaughter of their kinsmen, now commenced a skulking warfare upon all the tribes friendly to the French. Ever known as the "Firebrands of the Northwest," they became the veritable Ishmaelites of the wilderness. At every ford and portage, and by every stream used as a highway, lurked the savage Foxes with death in their hands. Into this vortex the Sacs were drawn. No French trader dared appear unprotected in all that territory. Time and again expeditions were sent out against them from Canada, and these were joined by warriors from every other tribe in Wisconsin, eager for the extermination of the common enemy. In the meanwhile a part of the Sacs had withdrawn from Green Bay to the Wisconsin River, and gave their name to Prairie du Sac; while some of the Foxes established a village at the mouth of that river. It was not in contempt that the Foxes were here known as the Dogs; and the French name, Prairie du Chien, Prairie of the Dogs, perpetuates the memory of their long residence here. As late as 1763, their village at Prairie du Chien was more substantially built and provided with evidences of a higher civilization than any other Indian town in the Northwest.

But even after the calamity at Detroit and the subsequent contests with all the neighboring tribes, the Firebrands, still unquenched, kept up the warfare until even their allies and kinsmen, the Iroquois, turned against them and joined with the other tribes in driving them from the Wisconsin.

It was not until 1736, when the subdued and chastened war party of the Foxes was reduced to sixty or seventy warriors, that they took refuge with their allies, the Sacs, beneath the shadow of the Watch Tower on Rock River.

7. "They all descended Rock River." Not all of them at once, as shown by the preceding note. There never was a time when all the Sacs and Foxes lived at the Watch Tower. Each tribe had villages more or less permanent in different parts of Wisconsin, Michigan, Illinois, Iowa, and Missouri. The Foxes had an important village at Davenport, another at Princeton, Iowa, and still another not very far from the mouth of the Wapsipinicon. As

shown in the preceding note, they were long established at Prairie du Chien, while both Sacs and Foxes had villages at the lead mines near Galena. The closest allies of the Sacs had their village at Moline. But Sauk-e-nauk was the metropolis of the allied tribes, and the largest Indian town on the continent.

8. "The Merrimac" is a small river flowing into the Mississippi south of the Missouri.

9. Soon after the purchase of Louisiana, Lieut. Zebulon M. Pike was appointed to conduct an expedition to the head waters of the Mississippi. He left St. Louis on August 9, 1805, with a party of about twenty men. He arrived at St. Louis in May, 1806. He did not visit Saukenauk, but met the Indians at their small village a little below the site of Davenport. His map locates the Sac village on the south side of Rock River, where Milan now stands. Not long afterward Lieutenant Pike made another tour resulting in the discovery of the Colorado peak which bears his name. On April 27, 1813, while in command of an expedition against York, now Toronto, Canada, he was killed by the explosion of a magazine.

10. "Some moons after this." Black Hawk clearly errs in the sequence of events, since Pike descended the river in the spring of 1806, while the murder of the Americans occurred in the spring of 1804. The American version of the story current at the time was, that a party of three Americans who had settled or were in camp near the Missouri River, had been attacked by a war party of Sacs and massacred. The leader of this party was a relative, a brother, it is said, of Quash-qua-me, the chief mentioned in the narrative. General Harrison, afterwards President of the United States, at that time Governor of Indiana Territory, whose jurisdiction had recently been extended to cover the newly acquired District of Louisiana, sent Captain Stoddard to the Rock River village to de-

mand the malefactors. The leader of the party above mentioned, whose name is unknown, voluntarily assumed the whole responsibility for the crime, and surrendered himself to General Harrison at St. Louis. The sequel of the story is told by Black Hawk.

11. "The country ceded by these four individuals." In June, 1804, President Jefferson instructed General Harrison to obtain cessions of territory from the Sacs and Foxes. It is not supposable that either Jefferson or Harrison intended to cheat the Indians out of that vast stretch of country, which in natural beauty and in agricultural and commercial possibilities is not surpassed on the globe. Meager as the price seems to be for upwards of fifteen million acres of land, yet excepting for the sentimental reason that the area about the Watch Tower had been the home of the tribe for generations, it was not altogether a bad bargain. The buffalo, deer, bear, and other large game which tempted to the chase, had long since disappeared. The fur-hunting trapper might delight in the beaver, mink, fox, and other small game in which the region abounded, but the elastic and irrepressible Sac found quarry much more to his liking in the vast wilderness north of the Missouri. Many of the tribe were therefore more than willing to exchange land of little value to them, however great the area, for a cash consideration and an annuity quite equal to all they had been making out of the land. But however little they may have valued the fertile lands to the east and south of them, they were united in the resolution to retain the little peninsula between the Mississippi and the Rock River, their ancestral home, the most beautiful, the most secure, the best beloved spot on earth to them. When it was discovered long afterward that Quash-qua-me had allowed it to be included in the cession, he was, as Atwater tells us, degraded from his rank as chief. Yet because they believed that he had been the victim of a fraud, they

gave him the consolation of conferring his former dignity upon Ti-a-ma, his favorite son-in-law.

12. "The origin of all our serious difficulties with the whites." Article II of the treaty bearing date November 3, 1804, between Gen. William Henry Harrison and the chiefs mentioned in the narrative of Black Hawk, reads as follows:

"The general boundary line between the land of the United States and the said Indian tribes, shall be as follows, to-wit: Beginning at a point on the Missouri River opposite to the mouth of the Gasconade River; thence in a direct course so as to strike the River Jeffreon at the distance of thirty miles from its mouth and down the said Jeffreon to the Mississippi; thence up the Mississippi to the mouth of the Ouisconsing River, and up the same to a point which shall be thirty-six miles in a direct line from the mouth of the said river, thence by a direct line to the point where the Fox River (a branch of the Illinois) leaves the small lake called Sakaegan; thence down the Fox River to the Illinois River, and down the same to the Mississippi. And the said tribes for and in consideration of the friendship and protection of the United States which is now extended to them, of the goods to the value of $2,234.50, which are now delivered, and of the annuity hereinafter stipulated to be paid, do hereby cede and relinquish forever, to the United States, all the lands included within the above described boundary." This boundary is shown in the map on page 12.

Article III provides that the United States shall annually deliver to the said tribes, at St. Louis, or at some other place convenient on the Mississippi River, goods to the value of $1,000, $600 of which are intended for the Sacs and $400 for the Foxes.

The region north of the Rock River above the prophet's town belonged to the Winnebagoes, and the country southward belonged to the Pottawattomies. The Sacs and Foxes did not claim ownership or possessory rights there, thus largely reducing the amount of land actually relinquished by the Sacs and Foxes under the treaty of 1804. It was at most no more than a quitclaim deed for whatever rights of possession they might at any time set up. The chiefs always claimed that they had never understood that they were disposing of any land north of Rock River. In 1816, Quash-qua-me said to Gov. Ninian Edwards, as he repeatedly had said before, "You white men may put on paper what you please, but I tell you again, I never sold my lands higher up the Mississippi than the mouth of Rock River."

Nevertheless, although it slowly dawned upon the Indians that these four men, without the sanction of a general council of the tribes, had presumed to dispose of all the land claimed by them east of the Mississippi River, and that the United States had accepted the cession and intended to enforce its terms, they looked hopefully to the Seventh Article for the security of their possession:

"Article VII. As long as the lands which are now ceded to the United States remain their property, the Indians belonging to the said tribes shall enjoy the privilege of living and hunting upon them."

In this article was concealed the final grievance of the Sac Indians. They did not understand how the United States could relieve themselves of the stipulation contained in that article, by selling the land to individuals. The idea of an absolute property in land vested in an individual seems never to have taken possession of the aboriginal mind. He held by occupancy only. He could not confer a title either feudal or allodial, because he never had it to confer. Such titles are the creature of law, and his laws never created them. He was quite unable to comprehend the legal and moral hairsplitting by which the United

States government, although precluded from disturbing his possession, could give one of its own citizens the right to oust him, while that government still claimed sovereignty. Black Hawk never could understand it; and it is quite doubtful whether you or I can.

13. "They were building a fort." Fort Madison, erected in 1808, by Lieut. Alpha Kingsley, in command of about sixty men.

14. "Killed like the British soldiers at Mackinac." In honor of the king's birthday, Captain Etherington, in command of the British fort at Mackinac, was keeping June 4, 1763, as a holiday; and in consequence had considerably relaxed the discipline of the post. The Chippewa Indians had notified Captain Etherington that as a special mark of loyalty to the English king and people, they had planned a game of baggattiway, or Lacrosse, with a party of visiting Sacs; and invited him and his garrison to witness the sport. In baggattiway, the favorite Indian ball game, a goal at each extremity of the ground marked the respective stations of the rival players. Each player used a bat about five feet long, with a hoop net large enough to hold the ball. Besides the garrison, many of whom had assembled outside to watch the game, all the squaws of both tribes were seated near the gate of the stockade. Although the day was unusually warm, each squaw wore a blanket. The game was opened when the umpire threw the ball into the center of the field. Immediately came the wild contest for its possession; the object, as in football, being to drive or carry it to the station of the opposing players. Sometimes the contestants closed together in dense groups struggling for the ball; and a moment later they were scurrying across the field in pursuit of it. Foot by foot, as the game proceeded amidst the boisterous shouts of excited players and absorbed spectators, the ball was ever nearing the open and practically unguarded gates of the fort. Suddenly

it was thrown almost within the entrance. The squaws, quickly rising, held out to the onrushing players the weapons concealed beneath their blankets; and an instant later, no longer players but fierce warriors, the Chippewas and Sacs swarmed into the fort and began the work of slaughter. Captain Etherington and Lieutenant Leslie were seized and carried away, to be released not long afterwards; but with few exceptions the British garrison and English traders were ruthlessly massacred. One of these traders, Alexander Henry, observing that the French residents of the fort were not molested, and were looking calmly on at the massacre, conceived the plan of finding security in one of their houses. Charles Langlade, a half-breed, who had led the Chippewas against Braddock in 1754, was Henry's friend and next door neighbor. Hastily climbing the low fence which separated their yards, he entered Langlade's house and begged to be concealed in a place of safety. But Langlade only shrugged his shoulders, and turned again to watch the massacre from his window. But a slave woman of Langlade's beckoned him to follow, led him to the garret, locked him in, and took away the key. He now secreted himself behind some birch bark vessels used in making maple sugar. How determined were the Indians upon the extermination of the English, may be seen in the fact that even Langlade's house was searched for their presence. The Indian woman had kept her secret, but another key was found, and four Indians entered the attic; but the darkness of the place prevented the discovery of Henry, and he had the joy of hearing the four savages descend the stairway

When the mad fury of the slaughter had somewhat subsided, the next day, Langlade, who had discovered or perhaps had always suspected the secret, fearing for the safety of himself and family, delivered him to the Indians. Through the intervention of some friendly chiefs, he was spared. He lived to tell the story in his "Travels and Adventures in Canada and the Indian Territories." He died in New York in 1824.

15. "The Shawnee prophet." This was Ellsk-wa-taw-a, the mischief-making brother of Tecumseh, who spoiled that great chieftain's plans by bringing on the battle at Tippecanoe during his brother's absence, before the formation of the great Indian confederation which Tecumseh was trying to establish. Many tribes had each its own prophet. Thus, the Winnebagoes had Powesheik, whose home was at the prophet's town on Rock River. He was the evil genius of Black Hawk, who seems to have had great faith in all sorts of prophets.

16. "We joined the last party." This attack was made on Fort Madison, September 5, 1812, at 5:30 p. m., and the siege was sustained by Lieut. Thomas Hamilton with less than fifty men until the evening of September 8th.

17. "We resumed our pastimes." With all the taciturnity and apparent gloominess of the Indian character, they were, among themselves, a most sportive and fun-loving people. Their games were mostly of an athletic nature, such, for example as ball-playing and horse-racing; and they were extremely fond of dancing. Most of these dances were a re-enactment around the council lodge of their battles and hunting trips. The warrior would come forward and go through the act of spying his foe. Crouching low to show craft and concealment, he would step with tense muscles around the circle in deadly and determined pursuit; then springing fiercely and suddenly upon the imaginary foe, engage with him in the last fearful grapple. Swaying, writhing, and panting in the intensity of the struggle, down went the vanquished Sioux with the victor's knife in his heart. With revengeful motions he would tear off his scalp, hold it aloft in triumph, dancing in short, stamping, staccato paces around the prostrate form. As

he left the stage amidst the boisterous applause of the assembled tribe, another warrior would enter the circle, and dramatically show the mode in which he had killed an enemy. Thus the dance went on, sometimes for several days with a most entertaining variety of movement and circumstance. But dances of this kind were not merely entertaining; they were regarded as highly instructive to the children and young men. "Here," says Black Hawk, "our warriors were made;" and he likens it to the military training which he witnessed at West Point. There was still another inspiration to these dances, and that was vanity and love of applause, which worthy traits the Indian shared in common with all other races. It was the only way he had of recording his exploits in the memory of his tribe.

"Among the Indians of the upper Mississippi," says Atwater, "the Sacs and Foxes are decidedly the best actors, and have the greatest variety of plays among them. Their war dances may be viewed as tragedies in the rudest state; and those dances wherein both sexes appear are truly comedies of no mean cast. Each person who acts is painted and dressed in a manner entirely appropriate for the part to be personated by the actor or actress. To see a play acted of a ludicrous cast of character, I have seen a thousand Indians present who were delighted with the acting. Thunders of applause followed some antic prank, while a visible displeasure would sometimes punish a failure to act well."

The Sacs were a generous people, holding property in very light esteem; and they felt quite well repaid for a gift or loan if they took it out of the recipient in some rough prank. It is said that the Foxes were at one time in need of horses, and sent a delegation of chiefs and warriors to Sauk-e-nauk to get them. They seated themselves in a circle while the young men of the Sacs went to bring them in. The young scamps soon came riding back, each carrying a switch. Around and around the circle dashed the young fellows in high glee, every now and then slashing away at the shoulders of their visitors, who, apparently oblivious to what was going on, smoked away in solemn silence. When the young Sacs had had their fill of the sport, they dismounted and presented the horses to the distinguished visitors.

Their game of ball has been already described under Note 14, where at Mackinac it was played as a cover for an intended massacre.

18. "They were attacked and defeated." The reference here is to the Fort Dearborn massacre on August 15, 1812. With this, the Sacs had nothing to do.

19. "Against a fortified place." Fort Meigs, on the Maumee River, where on May 1, 1813, General Proctor with a force of about 5,000 British and Indians, besieged Gen. William Henry Harrison. The soldiers who came down the river in boats were Gen. Green Clay's Kentuckians. One detachment of these pursued the British too far, and were defeated and captured, as Black Hawk says; but the other detachment was instrumental in raising the siege. The interference of Tecumseh and Black Hawk when the Indians were killing the prisoners, is well known in history. Tecumseh was under peculiar obligations to protect the white prisoners, having given General Harrison his promise that this should be done. At one time during the siege, the prisoners were undergoing rough treatment at the hands of the Indians while General Proctor was standing helplessly by. Tecumseh, riding up at the moment, leaped from his horse in great anger, and threatened to kill the first one who laid a hand upon the prisoners. "Why did you permit this?" he angrily demanded of General Proctor. "I am unable to restrain your warriors," was the reply. "You are not fit to command," cried Tecumseh; "go home and put on petticoats."

BLACK HAWK'S AUTOBIOGRAPHY 149

20. "The young war chief in command." Major George Croghan was only 21 years old when in command at Fort Stephenson (Lower Sandusky, Ohio). His garrison consisted of 160 men. On August 1 and 2, 1913, General Proctor attacked this post with 500 British regulars and 700 Indians. Major Croghan's defense of this fort and his repulse of the British and Indians, makes it one of the notable battles of the war of 1812. Their "success being bad and having got no plunder," Black Hawk left that night for his home with about twenty of his men. This was about two months before the battle of the Thames, where Tecumseh was killed. His departure was strictly in accordance with Indian notions of military discipline. "No success and no plunder" justified desertion at any time. A chief was obeyed not because of his office and rank, but because of his ability to lead his people to successful war.

21. "I have concluded to adopt him." This was Elijah Kilbourne, a native of Pennsylvania, who at the beginning of the war of 1812 was engaged as a scout. When Black Hawk started home on the night following the British repulse at Fort Stephenson, as stated in the preceding note, Kilbourne and a number of others were detailed to follow him and watch his movements. As they approached the vicinity of the village, the scouts, finding themselves in a situation of great peril, determined to separate, and let each man take care of himself as best he could. Just as Kilbourne emerged from a tangled thicket, he perceived an Indian on his knees drinking from a spring. Taking a quick aim with his rifle at the Indian, the hammer crashed down, shivering the flint into pieces without discharging the gun. In an instant Black Hawk was on his feet with his deadly aim directed at Kilbourne. Advancing toward his captive and ordering him to surrender, he marched him to his camp, a stone's throw distant. On the following

morning the Indians took their captive to the Rock River village, where he was adopted into the tribe as the son of Black Hawk, from which he was unable to escape for three years. No record has been left of his life among the Sacs.

22. "They forced us into a sink-hole." This affair, known as the battle of the Sink-hole, near Fort Howard on the Cuivre River, occurred May 24, 1815. The leader of the American troops, killed by Black Hawk at the first onset, was Captain Craig, and the white man killed at the edge of the sink-hole, upon whose body was placed the dead Indian, was Lieut. Edward Spears.

23. "On my return to Rock River." Here again Black Hawk errs in the order of events. The Sink-hole battle occurred in May, 1815, and the battle at Campbell's Island in July, 1814.

24. "One boat was drawn ashore by the wind." "During the night a strong wind came up and Major Campbell decided to take advantage of it and made an early start with his boats. When Black Hawk arrived at the Mississippi shore he found the Americans gone and he immediately started up the river in pursuit. Campbell's fleet had proceeded about six miles up the river beyond the island of Rock Island when they encountered a severe storm, which drove the boat commanded by Campbell upon the shore of the island, since known as Campbell's Island. While waiting for the storm to subside the troops landed and began preparing their breakfast. Black Hawk, who had followed on the Illinois shore, saw the stranded boat, and with his warriors he forded the Mississippi from the main shore to the island, and commenced an attack upon Campbell's soldiers. The two other boats which had preceded the ill-fated vessel, and which were commanded by Lieuts. Stephen Rector and Jonathan Riggs, hearing the report of fire-arms, quickly returned to the rescue. The

Bathing Beach Campbell's Island.

engagement lasted all day. The rangers effected a retreat after a heroic rescue of Campbell's crew, but left Campbell's ill-fated boat in the hands of the Indians, who, after plundering it, set it on fire. The total casualties were sixteen killed, of whom one was a woman and one a child. The Illinois legislature at its session of 1904-5 appropriated $5,000 for a monument to mark the spot." (From Hon. W. A. Meese's "Early Rock Island.")

25. "The boats arrived in the evening." The object of Campbell's expedition had been to reinforce the garrison at Fort Shelby (Prairie du Chien) or to recapture the post in case it had fallen into British hands. The failure of Campbell left the entire Northwest in practical control of the British. Moreover, as we have seen, the British, with great military sagacity, had supplied Black Hawk with cannon, skilled artillerymen, and plenty of ammunition. The instructions had been to guard this point at Rock Island, and to allow no American relief expedition to ascend the river. These instructions had reached Black Hawk just in time for him to intercept Major Campbell, whom he had a few hours before intended to allow to proceed on his way unmolested.

In view of these circumstances, an expedition was fitted out and left Fort Independence on August 2, 1814, reaching the mouth of Rock River on September 4 having the purpose of sweeping the country clear of this formidable band of Indians, and of establishing a fort in the very heart of Black Hawk's country, where that terrible chief could be held in control. The expedition was in command of Gen. Zachary Taylor, then Major Taylor, afterward President of the United States, with eight barges and about 400 men. Major Taylor found himself unable to ascend Rock River as far as Sauk-e-nauk, on account of the size of his boats and the low stage of water at that season. On the morning of September 5, the Indians commenced the attack, and the British with their cannon (Major Taylor's official report says they had one six-pounder, one four-pounder, and two swivels) soon compelled the American boats to drop out of their range. Taylor's report bears out Black Hawk's statement that "almost every shot took effect. The British being such good gunners, they rarely missed." Major Taylor held a council of war, and as they had but 334 effective men, officers and privates, to three times that number of the enemy, the expedition was abandoned and returned down the river.

26. "We met the great chiefs in council." These were Gen. William Clark, Governor of Missouri Territory, famous for his great explorations with Merriweather Lewis in the new Northwest; Ninian Edwards, Governor of Illinois Territory, and Auguste Chouteau, a prominent citizen of Missouri Territory, appointed by President Monroe as commissioners to conclude a treaty of peace and amity between the United States and the Sacs of Rock River. This treaty recited the fact that the Sacs had kept up the hostilities of the war of 1812 after the United States and Great Britain and all the other Indian tribes had long been pacified. After naming the different treaties to which the Sacs had been parties, including that of November 3, 1804, mentioned in Notes 11 and 12, the Sacs agreed to ratify and confirm them all. To this treaty Black Hawk "touched the goose quill," thus whether knowingly or unwittingly confirming the sale of the land for which he made war in 1832. This treaty was signed May 13, 1816. The Indians, however, were relying upon the seventh article of the treaty of 1804, by which they were to enjoy the privilege of living and hunting upon the ceded land as long as it remained the property of the United States. That is to say, the United States would never disturb their possession.

27. "A good spirit which lived in a cave." The mouth of this cave was on the north side of the Mississippi facing

Davenport. It is now closed by the abutment of the government bridge which spans the river at this point.

28. "We would then open the caches." These caches were made, so Judge Spencer tells us in his Reminiscences, by cutting out a circular piece of sod as large as would admit a man's body. This sod was laid aside and a hole dug, enlarging to a depth of five or six feet, so as to make it of a size sufficient to hold the corn, beans, squashes, and the like, of one family. The bottom and sides were lined with bark, and when the vegetables were deposited, they were covered with the same material. The hole was then filled up with earth. The circular sod was then replaced, and all the dirt removed so as to make it look as if the ground had not been disturbed. It depended upon the hiding whether there would be any provisions there in the spring; for they knew that as soon as they were gone, the Winnebagoes and other Indians would come and hunt for their treasure. These Indians, delving into the ground with their muskrat spears, often found the buried corn, and thus took the provisions of several families. These robberies never disturbed the pleasant relations between the tribes; but when a family had been thus despoiled, it was the custom to send some of the young men around the village, from one wigwam to another, and collect from each a small quantity for the benefit of the sufferers.

29. "This work was done by the women." The position of women among these Indians was not one of slavery, nor was their lot a particularly hard one. Housekeeping was not a very laborious task with them. If, for any cause the work of the women became burdensome, the husband solved the servant-girl problem by taking a new wife. The women seem to have made no objection to this arrangement, but in all the reported cases appear to have welcomed the newcomer as a valuable addition to the household. Marriages were intended to be permanent, and generally

were so; but when the parties found themselves uncongenial, they separated peaceably, and each was at liberty to seek a new mate. Although polygamy was allowed by their social code, it was rather unusual.

30. "I built my lodge on a mound." This lodge was at the place marked on the map on page 68 as "Graves of Black Hawk's Children." Just below it was Black Hawk's spring. This was a very abundant fountain long after the departure of the Sacs from Saukenauk; but it is now dry.

31. "I found a family occupying my house." This was the family of Judge Pence, and the time was March, 1829. Black Hawk was in an indignant mood, and said a good deal; but the only thing they could well make out, as Spencer tells us, was when Black Hawk pointed to the invaded wigwam, saying: "Sauk-e-wig-e-op;" and sweeping his hand about, said: "Sauk-e Auk-e;" by which they understood him to say that the wigwam and the land around it belonged to the Sacs.

32. "The one who remained." This was Joshua Vandruff. Among those who were not to be allowed to remain was Rinnah Wells. He was a resolute man, by no means disposed to be conciliatory toward the Indians. According to Judge Spencer, he had made it a practice to turn his horses and cattle out to pasture at night. These easily found their way through the frail fences of the Indians and destroyed their crops. Keokuk had gone to the settlers asking them to keep their cattle in at night, and they might turn them loose in the daytime, when the Indians would watch them and do them no harm. All had agreed to this excepting Wells, who turned his stock loose as before. That night the Indians rounded up Wells' cattle and turned them into his own well-fenced cornfield, and left them there. The next night Mr. Wells kept them in his barnyard.

33. "Afraid of the palefaced militia." The various troubles mentioned in the narrative and accompanying

notes, impelled the settlers to call upon the national and state authorities for help in removing the Indians. Accordingly, Governor Reynolds called for 700 volunteer mounted militia. About twice that number responded, and rendezvoused at Beardstown, under the command of General Duncan. They reached Rock River June 25, 1831, and crossed the south fork of that stream to Vandruff's Island. They believed that they were on the mainland, and were quite indignant to find that the main stream was yet before them. Meanwhile, General Gaines had come up Rock River a little above the foot of Vandruff's Island, his soldiers, amounting to ten companies of United States infantry, having been transported on barges. Meanwhile, a company styling themselves the "Rock River Rangers," consisting of about fifty men, for the most part settlers in that neighborhood, had started from Fort Armstrong toward the Indian village. All three of these parties finding that the Indians had departed from their village, believed that they had collected on Vandruff's Island. Gaines raked the lower end with grapeshot, and the rangers posted on the bluffs, with a few pieces of light cannon, made an ineffectual attempt to throw shot across the main stream of Rock River. But the Indians, as Black Hawk tells us, were miles away. General Gaines and the Rangers then quietly went back to Fort Armstrong. But the "palefaced militia" had come out to kill Indians, and, cheated of their prey, were determined to do something to repay them for their long march. When scows were brought to take them across the river, they fell upon the village, and although a thunderstorm was raging, they set fire to every wigwam, and marching to Rock Island, camped for the night. Thus fell Sauk-e-nauk. Both on that expedition and in the Black Hawk war of the following year, the militia were "under little restraint of their chiefs," and Black Hawk's belief that he would not be allowed to surrender, but that the tribe would have been given no quarter, was well founded.

34. "The British will assist you." Of course no responsible official at Malden held out to Neapope (Nawpope) any hope of assistance whatever. But he returned with his mind filled from some source with the crazy belief that the British were ready to lend their aid, and he so reported to Black Hawk. On his way back, he had stopped at the prophet's town, where that reckless dreamer assured him that the Pottawattomies and Winnebagoes were ready to unite with the Sacs and Foxes in driving the Americans from the Rock River valley. The prophet sent an urgent entreaty to Black Hawk to come to his village, raise a crop of corn, and perfect an invincible league of tribes, who, with the assistance of the British, would make them forever secure in the possession of their homes.

Around every fort on the border, from the earliest times onward, hovered a band of French, English, and American traders, in sharp competition for the rich furs and peltries of the Indians. No lie was too monstrous, no promise too plainly impossible of performance, with which to stir up the credulous Indians against their rivals. When the French and the British were in turn driven from the sovereignty of the Old Northwest Territory, the principal competition was between the British and American traders. The former government early lost all hope of regaining the country for themselves; but the traders, eager to overcome the natural advantage of the Americans (which they were throwing away by their uncompromising policy against the Indians), assumed a patronizing and friendly attitude toward the red man, while prodding him on to ill-will and deeds of violence against the Americans. One needs only to read the frank narrative of Black Hawk, to see how these traders went about it.

35. "The trader returned." Colonel Davenport had been to Washington, where he held an extended interview with President Jackson. The proposition to pay the In-

dians $6,000 to remove across the Mississippi, to which Black Hawk had reluctantly consented, was put before the President. The fiery Jackson would not listen to it. "I will not pay them one cent, Colonel Davenport," he cried; "they must go. By the Eternal, I will not pay them one cent!"

36. "We commenced our march up the Mississippi." This was, of course, in direct violation of the treaty made in the preceding June, shortly after the destruction of the Sac village, to which he had "touched the goose quill." Black Hawk had come to believe that treaties with the Americans were of no binding force whatever. The treaty of 1804 (See Note 12), "the origin of all our serious difficulties with the whites," had been made without any sort of authority on the part of the chiefs who signed it. Although Black Hawk and other chiefs and warriors, with the consent of the nation, had afterwards ratified it, it was with the belief that the Indians were to enjoy the privilege of living and hunting upon the territory as long as the United States owned it. This treaty of 1831, above mentioned, had been signed most unwillingly. The controversy between the peace party under Keokuk and the war party under Black Hawk, had diverted them from their usual winter hunting; their village had been burned and their cornfields seized by the white settlers, and the tribe was on the verge of starvation. Threatened with extermination by the militia under General Duncan and the regular troops under General Gaines at Fort Armstrong, he had yielded to the duress.

After crossing the Mississippi to the Illinois side opposite Fort Madison, he moved up that stream to the mouth of Rock River. As he proceeded up that stream toward the prophet's town, General Atkinson twice sent messengers after him demanding that he return and surrender. To each of these, Black Hawk sent a defiant refusal. But on reaching the prophet's town, a stunning disappointment awaited him. The Winnebagoes received him coldly and refused to ally themselves with him. He met with a like reception from the Pottawattomies. Entirely disillusioned, convinced that he had been deceived, and that his expedition was doomed to failure, he awaited only an opportunity to surrender. That opportunity came, as he believed, when he heard that Major Stillman, with a company of mounted men, had encamped about eight miles away. On May 12, Major Stillman and Major Bailey had been authorized to lead their battalions, amounting to about 275 men, some thirty miles northeast of Dixon, and coerce the hostile Indians into submission. On the 14th, Black Hawk was giving a "dog feast," a rare banquet and mark of respect, to some of the leading Pottawattomie chiefs, among whom were Sha-bo-na, Wau-ban-see, and others, staunch friends of the white men. How some forty of his men engaged in battle with the 275 well-armed and mounted militia; the violation of his flag of truce; the utterly panic stricken flight of Stillman's men, is all told truthfully in the narrative.

When Stillman's men reached Dixon after their wild flight before Black Hawk's "2,000 Indians," as they reported, there came a wild demand on the part of the remaining militia to be discharged at once. No persuasions, no threats, no pointing out that there were less than fifty Indians instead of the 2,000 which Stillman's men reported, could move them. They suddenly remembered the crops which they had left growing in the field; the families left at home undefended, and silently pleading for their valorous protection. Discharged they must be at once. Finding it useless to argue with men in their frame of mind, arrangements were made for mustering them out of the service, and Governor Reynolds at once issued a call for a new levy. They had come out for the fun of killing Indians; not for the grief of being killed, unless they could run faster than the redskins. It was at this time and under these circumstances that Capt. Abraham Lincoln's company of the fourth regiment, Illinois Mounted Volunteers, was mustered out at the mouth of the Fox River, on May 27, 1832, precisely one month lacking one day after they had been mustered in at Beardstown, Illinois. But Captain Lincoln and a considerable number of others had not shared in the panic. They had enlisted to do real military service and not to be bluffed out by the first shot. He accordingly re-enlisted as a private in Captain Iles's Company, organized for scouting service. As Black Hawk fled to the Four Lakes (Madison, Wisconsin), pursued by other troops, the new term of enlistment expired, and Captain Iles's company was mustered out for lack of further duties, on June 16, by Lieut. Robert Anderson, of Fort Sumter fame. On the same day, Captain Lincoln was again mustered into the service as a private in Capt. Jacob M. Early's independent company. This company was on constant scouting duty until July 10, when, provisions becoming scarce, the enemy retreating, and a general reorganization of the army having been determined on by General Atkinson, all the independent companies were mustered out, including that of Captain Early, to which Lincoln belonged. Always the last to leave a company as it was mustered out, and the first to re-enlist in another, his brief military career (April 28-July 10) was highly creditable. He always made light of his services in the Black Hawk war, but enjoyed telling the many humorous incidents of the campaign, in which he declared he "saw no live fighting Indians."

His itinerary in that war may be traced on the map on page 12 from New Salem, his home, to Beardstown; to the mouth of Rock River; to Dixon; Apple River; Galena; Stillman's battle ground (long after the battle); Pecatonica; Lake Koshkonong; to Dixon and thence home, partly by way of the Illinois River but mostly on foot. Belonging as he did in his last two enlistments to a scouting company, there were, of course, various side marches of no great length.

37. "He had once been a member of our tribe." Elijah Kilbourne, mentioned in Note 21.

38. "Two young white squaws." After Stillman's battle, when Black Hawk believed that he was to be denied the right to surrender, his flag of truce disregarded, and his envoys murdered, he at once began to plan for escape. His idea was to get to the Four Lakes, thence to and down the Wisconsin to the Mississippi and across that river, where the white man seemed desirous to have him go. The Black Hawk war, from the beginning, was apparently a determination on the part of the American troops to prevent the execution of this peaceable plan. If Stillman had received the two flag bearers, there would have been no war. It was a misunderstanding, of course; but the meaning of a white flag was perfectly understood by Black Hawk, and its violation on May 14 by the panic-stricken white troops admits of no excuse. The Indians, still anxious to escape, yet burning with indignation, separated into small bands and committed a number of murders. Some parties of Pottawattomies and Winnebagoes joined them; and saw in the turmoil the opportunity of avenging some of their private grievances. Among these was the massacre of the Hall family on Indian Creek, referred to by Black Hawk.

In 1830, William Davis, a blacksmith of powerful build and undaunted courage, built a cabin and blacksmith's shop on Indian Creek. Later, intending to erect a flour mill, he had commenced to construct a dam to furnish the necessary power. A band of Pottawattomies living some distance above the dam, objected to its construction, because it would interfere with their fishing. When the Indians attempted to destroy it, Davis was able to prevent them,

BLACK HAWK'S AUTOBIOGRAPHY   161

and in the quarrel, gave one of them a severe beating. Several white families had settled in the immediate neighborhood, among them William Hall, William Pettigrew, John and J. H. Henderson, Allen Howard, and others.

After Stillman's defeat, Shab-bona, the Winnebago chief, who for more than twenty years had been the unfailing friend and protector of the white settlers, knowing the existing temper of the Indians, mounted his pony, and dashing through the surrounding country, warned the whites of their awful peril. His son, Pype-gee, and his nephew, Pypes, were hastily dispatched to carry the warning to such settlements as were too far out of the way for Shab-bo-na to reach in time for their safety. Many of the settlements crowded together, and by uniting their forces saved them from attack. Some of the Indian Creek families fled to Ottawa, only to return in a few days, believing that the danger was over. Mr. Davis, however, brave and mighty, refused to seek safety, and made light of the warning carried by Shab-bo-na. His home, however, was open to such of his neighbors as chose to seek its shelter, and there were gathered there, in more or less fear and anxiety, a number of families, including those of William Hall and William Pettigrew.

From early in the morning on the date of the massacre, May 20, 1832, a band of about seventy Indians, Pottawattomies, Winnebagoes, and Sacs, had been hiding in the thick forest in the neighborhood of the Davis house, malignantly watching every movement made in the doomed settlement. So cautious were the movements of the Indians that not so much as the rustle of a leaf or the snapping of a twig betrayed their evil presence. About 4 o'clock in the afternoon, Mr. Davis, Robert Norris, Henry George, William Hall, and J. W. Hall, were in the blacksmith shop a few rods from the house; while half a dozen other men were working in a cornfield nearly half a mile away. William

Pettigrew, with the women and children, was in the cabin. The fierce barking of a dog suddenly attracted the attention of the inmates, and looking out of the open door, they saw the Indians in full war paint at the very threshold. "My God, here they are now!" cried Mrs. Davis. Mr. Pettigrew, with a baby in his arms, flew to bar the door, but was a second too late, and was shot down by the foremost of the savages, amidst the shrieks and cries of the despairing women and children, and the war whoop of the Indians. But the terror of the women and children was not for long. Hardly a minute elapsed before their despairing cries ended in eternal silence, as the tomahawks crashed through their skulls and the sharp knives of the red monsters pierced their hearts. One of the murderers, observing the infant which had fallen to the floor with Mr. Pettigrew, seized it by its little feet, took it thus into the yard and dashed its brains out against a stump. So sudden had been the attack and so overwhelming the force brought against them, that the men in the blacksmith shop had been unable to make an effectual resistance. The cabin was far too small to hold all the Indians, and the remainder had at once given their attention to Mr. Davis and his comrades. William Hall was shot at the first onset, and the others were dispatched almost before they could seize a weapon. Mr. Davis was the last to succumb, and the bloody circle around his dead body showed how heroic had been his last battle.

Meanwhile, the two daughters of Mr. Hall, Sylvia, aged 17, and Rachel, aged 15, were seized and hurried away to a camp of the Winnebagoes. Here arrangements seem to have been made for their return to the white people. After traveling about for nearly two weeks with the Indians, by whom they were treated with great respect, they were delivered under a flag of truce to the garrison of the little fort at Blue Mounds. It may be true, as Black Hawk believed, that the "two young white squaws" were spared through the intervention of the Sacs; but their murderous intentions against the others is clearly evident.

39. At the council held at Fort Armstrong in August, 1833, when Black Hawk was released, Major Garland made an address, in which Black Hawk understood him to say that he must obey Keokuk and conform to his counsels. Black Hawk rose in an excited manner and said: "I will not conform to the counsels of any one. I am an old man, my hair is gray. I once gave counsel to my young men. Am I to conform to others? What I said to our great father at Washington I say again. I will always listen to him. I am done."

40. After Black Hawk had completed his autobiography, as told in the introduction, he returned to his family on the Iowa River. The most distinguished man of his race, he was feted and feasted and flattered by Indians and white men alike; and this was dear to the old man's heart. In 1837, a delegation of Sacs and Foxes under the leadership of Keokuk went to Washington. Black Hawk accompanied the party. In the various cities visited, he was received with no less attention than on his first visit; but as he was not the official head of the party he kept himself in the background as far as he was permitted by the public.

On his return in the autumn, he built a cabin in Lee County, Iowa. In the following spring, he removed to the Des Moines River, near the spot shown on the map on page 12 as the grave of Black Hawk. Here, with his wife, Ash-aw-e-qua, the Singing Bird, the still beloved wife of his youth, his two sons, Nes-se-as-kuk and Na-som-see, the former said to have been one of the handsomest Indians ever seen, and his daughter, Nam-e-qua, he spent the last year of his life. General Street had made the family a present of a cow, greatly to their delight. The mother and daughter were model housekeepers; and it is said that they invariably wound up the morning's indoor sweeping and cleaning, by sweeping the yard in front of the cabin. As the warm days came on the flies became troublesome, it was their custom to sit down beside the cow and brush away the flies. In the midst of these pastoral scenes, the fiery old warrior was taken with bilious fever, and soon passed away. A few days before his death, Ash-aw-e-qua, who had been most devoted in her attentions to him, realized that the end was near. "He is getting old," she said; "Mon-i-to calls him home."

In July, 1839, Ash-aw-e-qua, weeping bitterly, informed Mr. Jordan, their friend, the trader, that the grave of Black Hawk had been opened and the body stolen. This ghoulish act was traced to a Dr. Turner. The bones had been cleaned and articulated when Governor Lucas discovered them, and were finally placed among the collections of the Burlington Geological and Historical Society. In 1855, they were consumed in a fire which destroyed the building and its contents.

THE END.

www.ingramcontent.com/pod-product-compliance
Lightning Source LLC
Chambersburg PA
CBHW050806160426
43192CB00010B/1664